ADVANCED PRAISE FOR *MADE IN THE USA*

During the days of slavery, abolitionists like Theodore Weld subpoenaed the conscience of the nation by having former slaves tell the horrific raw stories of their treatment. In like manner, Alisa Jordheim is shaking the status quo with the stories told by those formerly trafficked through sex slavery in this book. If you don't think human trafficking is happening where you live, think again! If you're concerned about this book disturbing your peace, remember, those bound in sex slavery have no peace. The truth makes us free, and may this book free us from denial and release us into action.

—*Will Ford*
Hilkiah Ministries

Ms. Jordheim's book is timely, emotional and grounded in research and personal experience. Through her words, the public sees how the pimps spot and then prey on our vulnerable children. But she doesn't leave us there, she draws attention to the preventive and restorative services that are necessary for children who are victims of commercial sexual exploitation."

—*Dr. Janice Shaw Crouse*
International End Demand Advisory Board,
Winner of U.S. State Department Abolitionist Award
and leader of Concerned Women for America's anti-trafficking work

Made in the USA is a compelling, heartbreaking, and breathtaking account of the lives that have been detrimentally affected by the travesty of trafficking. The factual connection of pornography being tied to trafficking is accurately portrayed in Alisa's real-life accounts. Until pornography is addressed widely in creating the demand for trafficking, a dent will never be made in tackling trafficking. I highly recommend that everyone read these tragic victims' stories, that are happening in our own neighborhoods. This is a worldwide problem now, in which everyone can help. Alisa's book captures exactly the reason why we do what we do.

—Tiffany Leeper
Founder of Girls Against Porn & Human Trafficking and
Chief Liberation Officer at The Gentlemen's Posse

Sex trafficking is a horrific crime that is increasing in our nation and globally. It is a topic that is difficult to read about and to discuss. But the reality is, all must gain understanding of this grievous issue in order that solutions can be discovered and the victims of this industry set free. In *Made in the USA*, Alisa Jordheim does an exceptional job of captivating the reader into the truths of the dark world of trafficking. While it is not easy to hear these stories, I encourage each of you reading this book to pass this message on to your family, friends, coworkers, and church family. Thank you, Alisa, for sounding a clarion call, for standing for freedom for these victims, and contending for justice.

—Rebecca Greenwood
President, Christian Harvest International
Author of Let Our Children Go

First of all, let me say...well done! This book will go far to serve as a warning to women and families across the United States. It is an incredible and detailed depiction of the horror thousands of young girls face daily across our country. I know this is a time of awakening for our country, and you have honored the victims depicted in this book. Their stories will save many.

—Rolando Lopez
Founder and CEO, Orphan Secure

MADE IN THE USA

The Sex Trafficking of America's Children

MADE IN THE USA

The Sex Trafficking of America's Children

ALISA JORDHEIM

~JUSTICE SOCIETY~

PUBLISHING & MARKETING, INC.

Oviedo, Florida

Made in the USA: The Sex Trafficking of America's Children
by Alisa Jordheim

Published by HigherLife Publishing and Marketing
400 Fontana Circle Building 1, Suite 105
Oviedo, Florida 32765
(407) 563-4806
www.ahigherlife.com

ISBN: 978-1-939183-40-8

Cover Design: Diane Vivian

First Edition
14 15 16 17 18 19 — 9 8 7 6 5 4 3 2 1
Printed in the United States of America

DEDICATION

This book is dedicated to my dear friend, H.S. You are the most

powerful, engaged, and authentic advocate with whom I have had the

privilege to work. Your heart for these precious children is unparalleled,

and it is a joy to watch you serve out of the purest motivation—

love. Thank you, my friend. You are an inspiration to many!

NOTE FROM THE AUTHOR

ALTHOUGH ALL INCIDENTS DESCRIBED in this book are true, some of the stories have been dramatized to convey the tragedy of child sex trafficking. Certain names, and in some instances other identifying characteristics, have been changed to protect victims' privacy and safety.

To maintain authenticity, all quotes have been left in the "slang" with which they were spoken.

Some material contained in the book is for mature audiences.

TABLE OF CONTENTS

PART III: SO YOU WANT TO MAKE A DIFFERENCE

ACKNOWLEDGMENTS

FIRST AND FOREMOST, I want to thank Deidra, Kate, Rich, Samantha, and Tiana. I am humbled to have walked with you, talked with you, and shared in your journeys. Your stories are the very heartbeat of this book. May your lives be richer for having been a part of this book. I know mine is.

To K.D., Lindsey, Luke, Philipa, and Stephanie, the five most gifted, young writing talents with whom I have had the privilege to work. You are amazing writers, and I have learned much from having worked with you. I especially want to thank you for the unique gifts each of you brought to the project:

- K.D.—Your commitment to truth and attention to detail.
- Lindsey—Your heart for the survivors and your team.
- Luke—Your beautiful, artistic writing style and your willingness to put it aside (a little) to write a linear story.
- Philipa—Your love of the craft and your willingness to jump in and help the other writers with your expertise.
- Stephanie—Your passion for becoming the very best writer you can be.

To Melissa and Lindsey, the most committed editors on the planet. After long hours of editing each story four to five times, you never gave in and never settled for a good story—you wanted the best. I am forever grateful for your friendship and partnership. The writers and I would likely agree that you are the reason these stories are great.

A big thanks to David, Laura, and the amazing team at HigherLife Publishing and Marketing. Your professionalism and care have developed this book (and me) to be the best ever. I consider you more than business partners—you are friends!

To my dear friends who carried this project deep in their hearts: Katie, Annette, Beverly, Lonnie, and Wendy. You kept me on task in heart and soul. Thank you for your love, friendship, and commitment to see this project through.

To Mom and Dad, you always said I could do anything. I believed you. Thank you for your love and support and for always being there.

To Errol, my precious son, you were my best and worst critic, and I loved it. Having you read the chapters, encourage me, and challenge me was a highlight of writing this book. I will remember your help and tell stories about it to your kids someday. You make my heart smile.

To Allan, my husband and partner in all things. You encouraged me to keep going when the nights got long, comforted me during those few crying jags, and strengthened me when the subject matter became too heavy to bear. Thank you. You are my rock, and I love you.

INTRODUCTION

UNDERSTANDING AND HOPE. THE purpose of this book is twofold: to bring understanding about how America's children are taken captive into the sex trade and to bring hope and light to one of the darkest subjects on the planet—child sex trafficking.

Most people think I'm a little unconventional. They ask me why I travel the nations to walk the "red light" districts, why I attend court regularly in support of kids giving testimony against their traffickers, and why I'm writing about this horrific issue. The answer: *I'm compelled.* Compelled to make a difference. And most importantly, compelled to make you aware that this crime is real and is likely happening on your campus and in your neighborhood this very minute.

Staggering, isn't it!? I'm faced with a challenge: How do I share such disturbing information and not leave you, the reader, feeling overwhelmed and despondent but, rather, hopeful and empowered that this inhumanity can be overcome? With that in mind, I entertained a number of ways to write this book. I could inundate you with statistics (boring), write from an expository approach (interesting), or take you into the hearts and minds of survivors through stories (captivating). I've chosen to captivate you with stories—true stories—of courageous adult survivors who were trafficked as children.

These stories are gritty and heartbreaking and, at the same time, riveting. Many of the scenes are difficult to read, and the language among the pimps, johns, and children is rough and sometimes profane. This is intentional.

My hope is that, after reading this book, you will understand the psychological and physical abuse these children face daily.

You can expect to experience a wide range of emotions as you read and associate with the vulnerability and fear of these survivors. I personally alternated between sorrow and outrage. I wept with many of the survivors during the personal interviews. Most of the writers and editors admitted to weeping while listening to the audio testimonies as part of the writing process. Tough stuff, but so worth it. And here's the best part—in the end, you will experience encouraging emotions such as thankfulness, joy, and amazement that each of these survivors has overcome and lived to share his or her story.

I have a personal saying when I am about to embark on a challenging endeavor: Strap in for Mr. Toad's Wild Ride—it's going to get bumpy. (For those of you who don't know what I'm talking about, Mr. Toad's was a crazy little car ride that made even grown-ups sick at Disneyland). So I say, strap in for a wild ride through the labyrinth of child sex trafficking in America.

Here's what you can expect from *Made in the USA*. The first two chapters will provide a global perspective on child sex trafficking, followed by the local issue in America. These chapters are by no means exhaustive (I will leave that to the experts) but are intended to give you a foundational understanding of the overall issues. Next come stories where things really get bumpy. To prepare you for each story, you will be given a short overview about the type of trafficking the story addresses. Each story wraps up with closing remarks directly from the survivor. The diversity of these stories is what makes *Made in the USA* so unique. I purposefully selected these five distinct tales to give you intimate insight into different captivity scenarios: Lover boy syndrome, familial trafficking, survival sex and male prostitution, recruitment, and kidnapping. Finally, you'll be given practical steps to join the fight through accounts of "normal" people who are making a difference to help trafficked children. That chapter is titled "You Don't Have to Be a Rock Star: Everyday People Making a Difference." While these people might not be rock stars to the world, they sure are to the kids for whom they're fighting.

Your willingness to read this book indicates that you are bold, brave, and living a little on the edge. Thank you for that. Many people cannot, do not, and will not acknowledge or discuss this difficult topic. You may need to take a breather between stories. It's OK. Each story is unique, so you would be doing yourself a disservice by reading only one. Take the time you need, and finish well. Allow the reading of this book to become a *labor of love* in honor of these exceptional survivors. The writers and I did, and we are so much better for it.

Congratulations—you already are making a difference. By purchasing this book, you are now a part of the solution to end child sex trafficking in America. All profits from the book will be given to recognized national organizations for the prevention and restoration of child victims of domestic minor sex trafficking. You might think of yourself as "just normal," but in my book, you have the makings of a rock star!

Part I

WHAT'S THE PROBLEM?

About two million children are exploited into the sex trade every year.

Chapter 1

KIDS FOR SALE: A GLOBAL VIEW

I brought children into this dark world because it needed the light that only a child can bring.

—Liz Armbruster, wife, mother, and grandmother

INDIA: SEVEN-YEAR-OLD SACHI AND her mother live together in a brothel in Calcutta. Because they share only one small room, Sachi is forced to stay under the bed while her mother is "servicing" customers. When Sachi is old enough, she will no longer be allowed to live in the small room free of charge but will be forced to service clients like her mom does.

Africa: Asabi is only ten. She walks into the brothel alone. She isn't too worried; she knows her mom will be waiting outside for her when she is "finished." In Asabi's culture, everyone must do what they can to help support the family—even if that means exchanging sex for money.

Ukraine: Karina is packing her belongings to leave the orphanage. She just turned sixteen and has "aged out" of the system. She knows the stories about orphanage employees alerting traffickers when girls are released, but what can she do? As she leaves the security of the orphanage, she will need to find food, work, and a place to live—all on her own. Alone and vulnerable, Karina is a prime candidate for being lured by a trafficker.

Cambodia: The village of Svay Pak is commonly referred to as a brothel village and has the disturbing reputation as a destination for sex tourism. It is rumored that foreigners take advertised sex tours to the village for the sole purpose of engaging in sex with children.

Photo: Alisa Jordheim, Svay Pak, Cambodia

"Buying sex with a twelve-year-old girl in Cambodia takes less time and effort than changing money in a bank or paying a telephone bill. ... [These kids spend their days in] shophouses where you will be offered "boom-boom"—sex—and "yum-yum"—oral sex—for five dollars a time in cramped, clammy rooms and makeshift plywood cubicles."

—A journalist from the streets of Svay Pak

USA: Maria was twelve when her dad left the family. Soon after, her mom started sleeping with men to bring in money. "I saw the men coming and going, but they didn't touch me. My room was safe." Maria said. "Safe until Mom started sending men to my room to have sex with me instead of her."

USA: "I hate you!" yells thirteen-year-old Shalonda as she runs out the door. Walking to the gas station just down the street, she meets "Selfish." In two minutes, he knows her name and every detail of the fight with her mom. "Hey, I know a way you can get some money and really make your mom mad," he says. That's all it takes—Shalonda agrees to go with him and enters into a life of commercial sexual exploitation.

USA: Carrie didn't know that Jill was a "plant" to lure her out of the youth shelter and into the hands of a trafficker. Jill seemed so interested in Carrie, asking about her family, friends, and even if she had a boyfriend. All of it was a setup to gain Carrie's trust in an effort to exploit her.

The stories are endless, the scenarios varied—but the problem is the same. Child sex trafficking isn't happening just "over there"—it's everywhere. About two million children are exploited into the sex trade every year.[1] This is a crime that affects every nation, including America.

Why is child sex trafficking growing so quickly? The global sex trade is big business—really big business. A Child Wise report on child sex trafficking shows it is the largest form of human trafficking in the world, with the majority of victims being young females between the ages of ten and eighteen.[2]

Why are children being targeted for commercial sex worldwide? Poverty, vulnerability, marginalization—there are a number of factors but no single answer. Each nation has its own set of cultural practices that, unintentionally, advance this crime. In some nations, children are marginalized, being valued only for what they contribute to the family. This devaluing leads many relatives to sell their children into the sex trade to provide income for the family. Child marriage is another potential cultural driver, with one-third of the world's girls married before the age of eighteen and one in nine before the age of fifteen.[3] Countries that have legalized child marriage are generally more lenient toward adults having sex with children. In some parts of the world that have high HIV infection rates, such as Africa, India, and the Caribbean, there is a dangerous belief that having sex with a virgin cures AIDS. This superstition is leading to the sex trafficking of babies and children for the practice of "virgin rape."[4]

> *"Sometimes our men in this culture have 'bad manners' and have sex with children."*
>
> —The head of social welfare in an African country[5]

Child sex trafficking in America might not be as visible as it is in some countries, but do not be fooled. It is a very real and growing problem in the United States—one that is not going away until we openly and honestly address the issue, and dispel the myth that American children are safe from commercial sexual exploitation. If we do not recognize the vulnerability of American children, a trafficker will.

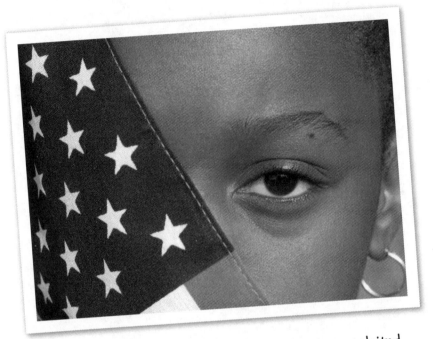

At least 100,000 American children are being exploited through pornography or prostitution every year in the United States.

Chapter 2

IN OUR BACKYARD: CHILD SEX TRAFFICKING IN AMERICA

"The only way not to find this in any American city is simply not to look for it."

—Ernie Allen, former president and CEO,
National Center for Missing & Exploited Children[1]

AMERICA—THE LAND OF THE free—doesn't seem to be so free these days. It is estimated that at least 100,000 American children are being exploited through pornography or prostitution every year in the United States.[2] It is hard to believe that with all of our modern advances, kids of every class, race, geography (urban, suburban, and rural), and socioeconomic status are falling prey to the horrific crime of child sex trafficking.[3]

What Is Child Sex Trafficking?

"With the young girls, you promise them heaven, they'll follow you to hell."

—Arizona pimp[4]

It's important that we take a moment up front to define a few common terms related to the sex trafficking of American children.

- **Child Sex Trafficking:** Any commercial sex act if the person is younger than eighteen, regardless of whether any form of coercion is involved.[5]

- **Commercial Sexual Exploitation of Children (CSEC):** Sexual activity with a child younger than eighteen in exchange for something of value—or the promise of something valuable (money, goods, services) where one or more parties benefits from the exchange.[6]

- **Domestic Minor Sex Trafficking (DMST):** The commercial sexual exploitation of American children within US borders.[7]

While these definitions are often used interchangeably, it is important to understand the differences. Child sex trafficking and CSEC can be used to identify both domestic and international victims, while DMST is specific to American children. CSEC is also the term most commonly used by law enforcement and government agencies.

For the purposes of this book, the terms commercial sexual exploitation of a child and domestic minor sex trafficking will refer to victims of child sex trafficking in America.

Who Are These Kids?

"We've seen young girls being exploited, and there's no common thread as far as black, white, Asian, upper class, upper-middle class, lower-middle class, poor, house, home, single, double. That varies."

—Sgt. Ernest Britton, Atlanta Police Department[8]

While any child can become a victim, there are several prevailing factors that make a child particularly vulnerable to commercial sexual exploitation: runaway tendencies, homelessness, poverty, limited education, history of sexual abuse, a parent or family member involved in prostitution, gender bias, sexual orientation discrimination, and mental disabilities.[9]

The average age for a girl lured into sex trafficking is twelve to fourteen; for boys and transgender youth it is younger, eleven to thirteen and some cases involve prepubescent children, toddlers, and babies.[10] The primary ways these kids are exploited is through street or Internet-based prostitution, strip clubs, erotic entertainment, and pornography.[11]

Our Sexualized Culture

"But a prostitute is someone who would love you, no matter who you are or what you look like. Yes. It's true, children."

—"The Prostitute Song," from an episode of *South Park*[12]

We live in a sexually charged culture that exposes young children to adult imagery, activities, and a normalization of commercial sex. The boundaries are blurring. Television content that once was reserved for late night is now mainstream, and youth can easily access adult video games and movies with one click. After checking the box that indicates you are older than eighteen, kids of all ages now have access to games such as *Pimpwar*, "where players become masters at the art of pimping hoes."

Sexuality and prostitution are not only being introduced to our children via media, but now even more blatantly through music, clothing, and toys. Here are just a few sexually explicit children's items that, after public outcry, have been removed from the market:

- A pole-dancing toy that, although marked "adult use," was listed on a children's toy website
- "Push-up" bikini tops for girls ages eight to fourteen
- Thong underwear with "Eye Candy" and "Wink Wink" for seven-year-old girls

Pole-dancing toy listed on a children's website, source unknown

One Chinese company developed a life-size child sex doll made to look like an Asian girl of eight to ten years old. It is purported that fifty-seven of the dolls sold at a price tag of $178 before their removal from the website. But there's more to the story in Chapter 8.

Child Pornography

"Unfortunately, we've also seen a historic rise in the distribution of child pornography, in the number of images being shared online, and in the level of violence associated with child exploitation and sexual abuse crimes. Tragically, the only place we've seen a decrease is in the age of victims. This is—quite simply—unacceptable."

—Attorney General Eric Holder, Jr., 2011[13]

The United States is the largest producer of pornography in the world. With 55 percent of all child pornography coming from America, it is a $3-billion-plus annual industry. One of every five pornographic images is of a child.[14] One of every five! While adult pornography is for the most part legal, child pornography is illegal and carries severe penalties for those involved. Anyone who knowingly views or produces child pornography is guilty of child sexual exploitation. Once it involves gain through a third party, it becomes child sex trafficking.

The US Department of Justice reports growing accessibility to child pornography by offenders. "[They] can connect on Internet networks and forums to share their interests, desires, and experiences abusing children, in addition to selling, sharing, and trading images." Disturbingly, there is also an increase in the sadistic and violent nature of the child images produced. It is very difficult to retrieve and eliminate pornography once it is posted on the Internet. This often compounds the humiliation and victimization many survivors experience, knowing that the images can be viewed indefinitely for the sexual gratification of predators.[15]

Changing Our Language

"I would rather be known as a murderer than a prostitute."

—Adult survivor[16]

I would like to make one thing clear: There are *no* child prostitutes.

A prostitute is commonly defined as an adult who consensually exchanges sex for money. Using the term prostitute in connection with a child can bring misunderstanding to the definition of child sex trafficking and implies that the child is making a choice. These children are not making choices. They are being exploited.

Let's take a look at this from a legal standpoint. No one younger than eighteen can legally consent to any form of commercial sexual activity; therefore, there is no basis for the concept of a child prostitute.

It is time to remove the stereotype that these are just "oversexed kids" making bad decisions. It is time to align our words with the truth: Children who are sexually exploited commercially are always, initially, victims of a crime.

The Rest of the Book

This book is intended as a guide to understanding the commercial sexual exploitation of American children. It is not intended to be the expert's manual on all things related to child sex trafficking. For those of you who want to dig deeper, a number of excellent resources are listed at the end of the book.

Because no child can legally work for a pimp, I have used the terms "pimp" and "trafficker" interchangeably throughout the book. The term pimp has foolishly been glamorized in our culture, giving the wrong message and doing a disservice to our children. When referring to the exploitation of children, every pimp is a trafficker. Additionally, in an effort to conserve space, I have used the term "girls" when referring to girls and boys throughout the text.

Now that you have had an introduction to the international and domestic drivers of child sex trafficking, it is time to move on to the stories. I encourage you to read these stories with a watchful eye, looking for any indicators that might be affecting your own family, friends, or community.

Part II

STORIES FROM
THE FIELD

Young girls usually form bonds with their exploiter who will pretend to be the girls' boyfriend.

Chapter 3

LOVER BOY SYNDROME

"He's not my pimp—he's my boyfriend."

—Trafficking survivor

SADLY, MANY TRAFFICKED GIRLS in the United States do not recognize their own victimization. This is a pimp's strategy from the beginning—to seduce the child into a one-sided relationship of complete submission and blind devotion to him.

What's a Lover Boy?

This trafficking tactic is known as "Lover boy syndrome" and is, by far, the most common approach pimps use to lure young girls into commercial sexual exploitation.

"We eat, drink, and sleep thinking of ways to trick young girls into doing what we want them to do."

—Chicago ex-pimp[1]

A Lover boy will target young girls who are defenseless and can be manipulated easily. Vulnerabilities traffickers look for in girls are low self-esteem, isolation, a history of sexual abuse, homelessness, a fatherless or broken home, conflict with parents, and other signs of insecurity.

> *"Any player can tell when a girl has the look of desperation that you know she needs attention or love. It's something you start to have a sixth sense about."*

—Chicago ex-pimp[2]

The primary means of control this type of trafficker uses is psychological manipulation. Lover boys are typically charismatic and persuasive, priding themselves on their ability to control young girls through finesse. Their tactics are systematic. First, they initiate conversation with the intention of drawing out the child's vulnerabilities. Next, they listen intently and develop a relationship based on the child's needs. Whatever she needs—father, boyfriend, or caregiver—that is what the Lover boy provides.

> *"He was able to lure me away from home with things like he could help me become a model, he could help me become a songwriter because I really wanted to join a rock band. Things that might sound not so real to an adult. They worked well on me at fourteen. And so he lured me away from home, and within hours of running away, I was forced into prostitution. ... "*

—Holly, survivor[3]

The Honeymoon Phase

The relationship will have an initial period of false love and feigned affection, which is known as the "honeymoon" phase. The bonding that occurs during this phase is critical to attaining long-term mind control over the child. Some bonding techniques traffickers use are gifts, compliments, sexual and physical intimacy, and promises of a better life.[4] As the relationship progresses, the girl becomes dependent on her trafficker to meet her physical and emotional needs. Once this dependency is developed, the Lover boy will ask the girl to help support him financially by any means necessary, specifically prostitution.

> *"A few months ago, seventeen-year-old Sarah was walking to the store alone. A thirty-year-old male drove up beside her and told her how pretty she was and asked why she looked so sad. Sarah told him that she was angry with her mom and just needed to take a walk. He asked if he could take her to get her nails done down the street to cheer her up, and she agreed. . . . They spent a lot of time together, and he asked Sarah to move in with him, but after a month of living together, he told her he couldn't make the rent payment and needed help. He asked her to go on dates with older men and engage in commercial sex. Sarah felt uncomfortable, but agreed because she would do anything not to return home and wanted to make him happy."*
>
> —Sarah, survivor[5]

Trauma Bonding

Once a girl has been "turned out" by exchanging sex for money, the relationship changes. The honeymoon phase soon ends, and the trafficker typically becomes verbally and physically abusive, forcing her into continued prostitution. She is confused by the loss of affection and will do anything to get back her trafficker's love and attention. This connectivity between the victim and the trafficker is called "traumatic bonding" and is similar to Stockholm Syndrome. Traumatic bonding is a "strong emotional tie that develops between two persons, where one person intermittently harasses, beats, threatens, abuses, or intimidates the other."[6]

> *"Weakness is the best trait in a person you want to control. You have to tear down someone's ego to nothing before they will start looking to you for salvation."*

> —Pimpin' Ken[7]

Despite this abuse, the child becomes brainwashed into believing she has chosen a lifestyle of prostitution and is in complete control of her own life—fully convincing herself that she is *not* a victim.

When a girl has resigned to or even embraced a lifestyle of sexual exploitation, she will likely conform to the "rules" required by her trafficker to please him. Pimps often require girls to write and recite the rules they are to live by. Police found a handwritten collection of rules in Carlton "Privilege" Simon's car when he was arrested on suspicion of promoting prostitution in 2006.

Rules 2 Da game of Hoez !!!

1) Always make them need and depend on you So you have Power over them. (Power is control)
2) Make them understand that you don't need them they need you, and they are reMiserable. Never let them no if you need them deep down inside.
3) Never let not get away with sneakin anything Cause once they feel they can get away they will always

Pimp rules, Suffolk County Sheriff's Office

RULES TO PIMP HOME

> *"Rule #7: Be down and dirty, side or die for your pimp, even if it involves sacrificing yourself. Your pimp is your priority, your primary, and your number one, and you are to see to his every need."*

> —Privilege, a pimp[8]

On Automatic

While flying into Dallas, Texas, for the 2011 Super Bowl, an anti-trafficking associate of mine overheard one pimp talking to another on the airplane.

He said something to the effect of, "Most of the girls flew in last night and are waiting for me to arrive. We will do good business. We are bringing in *carne fresca* (fresh meat) for the game." This pimp's victims were clearly "on automatic" and didn't even need him in the same city to stay "dutiful" to him.

Once a girl has reached this degree of bonding with her trafficker, she will seldom attempt to run away. He and the other girls have become her support system. She will either "love" him and choose to stay under his control, or she will be too fearful of being on her own to leave. This bonding creates a mechanized return response in the girl. Even if she has an opportunity to leave, she will choose to come back to her pimp. This is known as being on automatic.

"The process of sending girls on automatic allows the trafficker to keep a distance from the crime he is committing."[9] Keeping her isolated from others outside of the pimp "family" and dependent on the family to have her needs met ensures that she will remain on automatic. In the words of one hardened pimp:

> "One of the best ways to keep a ho off balance is to move her around. If a ho is in a location too long, she will get used to the place, and her mind will wander to her own thoughts. ... Without roots, even the mightiest tree can be easily moved here and there. People are the same way. Without strong ties to a place, family, or loved ones, they can be easily manipulated and controlled. If you can keep a person off balance, they'll be too busy trying to regain stability to try to unbalance you."
>
> —Pimpin' Ken[10]

Physical and Psychological Effects

Denver Police Department and Prism magazine, progression of eighteen-year-old girl prostituted over a period of one year.

"He'd make me go stand out on the street until a trick would pick me up. Sometimes it was dangerous, but I knew he cared about me, 'cuz he said he'd buy me a Taser once I earned enough money to afford one."

—Survivor, age fourteen

Sex-trafficked children are losing more than just their innocence. They are being robbed of their very lives. Tragically, most trafficking victims will die within seven years of first being trafficked. An average woman may live to be eighty-one years old and a man seventy-six, but these children can expect to die at an average of twenty to twenty-one years old.[11]

"You start by making rules for yourself, but if you're out there and you're not getting the money you want, you can start giving in [unprotected sex]."

—Youth survivor[12]

It is important to emphasize that commercially sexually exploited children suffer from a number of serious physical ailments. They more readily engage in unsafe behaviors such as "raw," or unprotected, sex to make more money. This makes them highly susceptible to HIV and AIDS. Sexually exploited children also are exposed to excessive forms of violence, including bondage, dominance, and sadomasochism, known as BDSM, along with snuff or splatter films, which often include the actual violent death of a participant engaged in a sex act. Along with these disturbing realities, there are other abuses from which trafficked children might suffer, including:[13]

- Sexually transmissible infections
- Drug and alcohol addiction
- Malnutrition
- Sterility, miscarriages, and menstrual problems
- Physical injuries such as broken bones, burns, and vaginal and anal tearing
- Traumatic brain injuries, including concussions
- Death

"Prosecutors allege that he [pimp] kept a new pair of Timberland boots in his car that he would put on and use to stomp a prostitute."[14]

For those fortunate to live through the abuse, many will suffer short- and long-term psychological effects from the trauma:[15]

- Depression or hopelessness
- Low self-esteem
- Anxiety
- Insomnia
- Extreme grief
- Fear

- Dissociative disorders
- Suicidal thoughts and behaviors

Becoming a Bottom

A natural progression for a girl who has been with a pimp for an extended period of time is to become his "bottom." The role of a bottom is considered to be a position of power and status over the other girls under the pimp's control. She might be required to handle finances, train and recruit other girls, work the track (common prostitution areas) in her pimp's stead, run interference for and collect money from the girls under the pimp's control, and look after the pimp's affairs if he is out of town, incarcerated, or otherwise unavailable.[16] Having become solely devoted to her pimp, a bottom will assume a defensive role to protect her trafficker.

> *"When he went to prison for ten years for almost killing one of his girls, she took over the business to raise money for his attorney fees."*[17]

—Bottom girl

Most girls regret that, in their role as bottom, they participated in the recruitment of other unsuspecting victims. While the girls have clearly been victimized initially, after time, they become desensitized to the life, and some assume positions as bottoms, recruiters, and even traffickers themselves. This seems to be an area of great shame for many women who have been prostituted. In the next story, you will witness Tiana's progression into the role of bottom alongside her trafficker.

After all of this sobering information, it's time for a little inspiration. There are so many wonderful stories of men and women who have not only come through being trafficked but are now powerful leaders in the fight. They didn't transition from being held captive to leadership overnight. They each had their own journey of overcoming, step by step.

These next two sections, titled "There Is Hope" and "The Inside Story," appear at the end of each overview. There Is Hope will give you a brief tale about a survivor or advocate, and The Inside Story will give you a small fact about the survivor whose story you are about to read.

There Is Hope

"Jazmine was waiting to interview for work at the strip club. She had been sleeping on the streets, turning tricks for an abusive 'boyfriend,' and was desperate for help. So a friend and I made some calls. The one home that would take her demanded that she leave her cigarettes and drugs behind. She had a BIG decision to make. Did she really want out of the life or just a short break from the streets? Time would tell. I dropped her at the home—but didn't know if she stayed. Months later, I unexpectedly ran into Jazmine. After big hugs, she said, 'It isn't easy, but I'm still at the home and taking it one day at a time.' Jazmine stayed and was taking steps toward freedom—now, I call that success!"

—Alisa Jordheim, Founder, Justice Society

The Inside Story

"It was a victorious and painful day for Tiana, as she sat in my living room sharing the details of her captivity. This was the first time she had put her experiences into words. The retelling was difficult, and we cried a lot that day, but Tiana was committed to have her story told. She believes that if sharing her story will help keep one girl from falling prey to a 'Lover boy,' then it is worth telling."

This is what Tiana had to say after reading her own story for the first time: *"Wow!!!!! Alisa, I can't tell you how overwhelming it was to read that. Not in a bad way at all, just kind of surreal. I love it."* The following story is Tiana's courageous journey from captivity to freedom.

NO PLACE TO CALL HOME
By Lindsey T. Nunn

I sit alone on my bed in my grandma's trailer looking out at the Alabama sunset. It's that moment during dusk when the sunlight is a deep yellow just before turning orange and disappearing. Watching the dust float in the sunlight streaming through the blinds of my window, I think, *Grandma would be cleaning now if she were here to know how dusty it is.*

I shake myself out of my dreamy state to look around my room for the last time, pick up my one small bag of possessions, and say goodbye to the only place I've ever been loved. Taking a deep breath, I inhale the smell. Grandma's trailer always smells so clean. *Goodbye, home.*

I feel sadness overwhelm me again, and I want to lie down and cry. *There's no time for that. Grow up, Tiana. You've cried enough, and there's nothing you can do to change this. You have to take care of yourself now. ... But how?* My aunt is taking me in at her assisted-living apartment, just until after Grandma's funeral. She's allowed to have guests for only few days at a time, so after that, who knows where I'll end up?

I manage to get through the funeral without a total meltdown, and after one day with my aunt, I still have no ideas on where to go. I decide to call Mom. I know she's been too consumed in her grief and drugs to be worried about me. But I don't have anywhere else to go, and it won't hurt to ask if

I can stay with her a while. The phone rings. I bite my nails, waiting. She answers.

"Mom? It's me."

"Wha's it, Tia? I'm busy righ' now." Her words slur.

"Well, I just wanted to ask if maybe I could come stay with you a while? I won't have anywhere to stay in a few days, and I could come help… "

"How can you ask me that, Tia? You thin' I need one more thing to think abou'?"

Ugh, she can't even let me finish talking! Deep breath. "I know, Mom, but I won't be any trouble, and I'll help out, and you won't even know I'm there. I just need… "

"Tia, thire's too much goin' on righ' now. I juss got through yur brother's funeral an' then had ta plan yur gran'ma's. I don' have the money ta feed myself. I can' feed you, too. I'm sure you can fine a frien' or someone ta stay with. I'm sorry." She hangs up.

Why did I even try calling her? I knew she wouldn't want me. She never wanted me. Her life has always been consumed with drugs and taking care of my little brother, Tyler. He had muscular dystrophy, and Mom gave everything to care for him. That's part of why I left when I was a kid to go live with Grandma. Mom couldn't handle taking care of me, too. She catered to Tyler's every need for years and years, even damaging her shoulders to the point of needing surgery because she had moved his heavy, limp body around by herself so often. I thought maybe—just maybe—things would be different now.

A couple of weeks ago, ten days before Grandma died, Tyler's heart gave out. It was unexpected, and I know Mom blames herself for his death. She still can't manage to think about anyone but herself and him. And I've still got no place to call home.

It's my junior year of high school, and I want so badly to graduate with my class. The next several weeks, I hop from one friend's house to another[*], trying to stay in my school district and keep up in class. But it's hard to focus on homework and projects when I'm on the move all the time.

One night, when I'm trying to find the next place to move to, my friend, Alexis, comes to mind. I haven't talked to her since she dropped out of school a few months ago when her mom died. I text her and ask if she has room for me to crash with her for a while. She texts back right away: "Ti! Yeah, girl, come on! I haven't seen you in so long! I'm staying at the Motel 6 and am bored as hell over here."

I meet up with her in front of the motel where her boyfriend, Bruce, pays for her room. She squeals when she sees me.

"Oh, my god, finally someone to have some fun with! Bruce has been so grumpy lately, and I've been so lonely. Did I tell you he's married?"

"Um...no."

"Yeah, he keeps saying this place is our little getaway, but that soon he's gunna leave his wife for me. I just wish he'd leave her *now*."

She puts on a pouty face, but then smiles: "You and me'll have a great time, though!"

She locks arms with me, and we walk up to the room.

"So tell me, what's up with you?" she says. "Are you dating anyone?"

Memories of living with my mom and seeing her with naked men flash through my mind. I can't imagine why someone would want that. I've never even kissed a guy, and that's fine with me.

I smile at Alexis. "You know me! I never have time for boys."

---

[*] Couch surfing: Homeless youths' temporary utilization of the home of a friend, family member, or acquaintance for a place to sleep. A common situation in which minors are commercially sexually exploited.

"Well, maybe you will now," she says with a wink. "You're not going back to school, right?"

I'm not sure how to answer her. I've tried so hard for so long to stay in class and make it to graduation, but it just isn't working.

"For now, I think I'll take a break. At least until things are more stable. Maybe I'll go back next year to finish."

The room Alexis and I stay in isn't bad. There's a microwave where we cook TV dinners, and a maid comes every few days to clean and change the sheets. It's nice having a friend around, although Alexis mostly just talks about Bruce and the latest fight they've had.

After a couple of weeks, Alexis says to me, "So, I have this friend Chris who's really fun. He said we could stay with him for a while. He has all kinds of connections." I'm not sure what she means by "connections," but I figure if it's a place to stay, I'll go along.

"OK, sounds cool. What about Bruce and the room?"

"Don't get me started. I'm so sick of him! I'm not even telling him where we're going. He thinks just because he gives me money that he can keep me here, ready to put out at his command. He's never gunna leave the dirty slut he's married to, but I can get any man I want and any *thing* I want. He'll be pissed when he finds out I left right after he paid for this room another week!" She laughs.

The next day, Alexis drives us about twenty minutes to another town and parks in front of a dilapidated apartment building.

"Is this where Chris lives?" I ask. I guess my face shows my disgust because she responds:

"Oh, come on. It'll be more fun than it looks. I promise."

Once inside, I really wonder what Alexis means. Chris's apartment hardly has any furniture, and it's dirty. The smell of mold hits my nose, and I'm immediately nauseated. There's a small crowd of people lounging around, but it still feels lonely. Chris opens his fridge and says, "I'd offer you a drink, but…" His fridge is empty except for one beer. He takes the one beer for himself, and we sit down on the filthy couch that has a card table in front of it. There are rows of white powder on the table.

"Told you it would be fun," Alexis says.

What the… No way. I can't do this.

"Your friend looks kinda freaked," Chris says. "Not gunna wuss out on us, are you?"

"Oh, she's fine. Just got a little car sick on the way here," Alexis lies. She leans over to me and whispers, "Don't bail on me. It's fun, I promise. Besides, you can't knock it 'til you try it."

Right now, that statement doesn't make sense to me, but these people are my meal ticket, and I have nowhere else to go. *Maybe it will be fun?* I take my first line of coke.

We stay the night, and the next day I feel awful. I'm never doing coke again. I walk out of the bedroom I slept in, and Alexis, Chris, and a few other guys are gathered around the card table talking. I sit on the couch, listening to what they're saying. I don't know if it's the aftereffects of the coke or the smell of mold, but I feel like throwing up.

"These Asian guys came into town on some kind of business yesterday. They let me know they want some girls tonight," says Chris's friend.

"Perfect," Chris says. "I know just the girls. I'll send 'em over tonight."

He bags up a hit of cocaine and hands it to the other guy in exchange for a wad of bills.

I am freaking out inside. After living with Grandma for so long, I realize I've been really sheltered—I've never heard talk like this. My mom may have been an addict and even slept with guys for money, but she didn't discuss it in the open like these guys are.

I try to keep cool, like Alexis. I don't want them to know I'm scared as hell. I have to leave this place. Slowly, I stand up, head to the bedroom, and start packing my stuff. Hopefully, I can just walk out the door without them noticing and catch a bus out of here. I'm headed for the front door when one of the guys sees me.

"Where is she going?" He sounds panicked. "We can't just let her leave! She'll go to the cops!"

"I'm not going to the cops," I say, trying to stay calm. "I feel sick and just want to go home." Whatever that means. "Look, I promise, I'm not telling anyone what's going on here. Just let me leave, and I won't tell anyone."

Chris looks paranoid. "Grab her bag!" One of the guys does.

"Whatever, keep it," I say. "I don't care."

I swing the door open and start running. They don't come after me. Not even Alexis. My heart is racing, and I'm running as fast as I can. I make it all the way to a gas station two blocks away before I realize I don't even have my ID. My clothes, shoes—everything I own except the clothes on my back—are in my bag. At least I have enough money in my jeans pocket for the bus.

My great-aunt, the same one I stayed with before Grandma's funeral, should be able to put me up again. That will buy me some time until I find another place to go. A lady at the bus stop lets me borrow her cell phone to call my aunt. This time I can stay with her for a week, and that's more time than I thought I'd have.

Three days pass at my aunt's, and I still don't know what I'm going to do. Maybe I can go back to stay with Alexis. I don't think she was staying long-term with that guy Chris—that was just a short stay. She seems to always be looking ahead to her next step. I text her.

"Hey, grl, just wondering if you know of a place I can stay? Im at my aunts and only have a few more days I can stay here."

"Grl u calmed down since the last time I saw u? I'm in Atlanta with this guy Marcus. Hes got room for anthr grl. He'll give u a job n take care of u. Give him a call. Hes real nice."

She texts me the number, but I'm not sure what I want to do with it. As I crawl into bed, I start thinking over my options. It doesn't seem smart to go stay with a guy I don't know in another state. On the other hand, a job sounds great, and Alexis said he's nice. I've never been to Atlanta, let alone a state other than Alabama. It's gotta be better than what I have here— nothing. *What choice do I have? I really don't have any options. I have nowhere else to go.* In a few more days, I can be either on the streets or with this guy, Marcus, starting a new life. The next morning, I call the number.

"This is Marcus."

"Hi, this is Tiana. ... I'm a friend of Alexis's. I'm looking for a place to stay, and... "

"Oh, yeah, Alexis told me about you. Baby, you're in Alabama?"

I feel shivers go down my spine. I've never been called "baby" by a man.

"Yeah. I don't really have a way to get to Atlanta, though."

"Don't you worry about that. I'll take care of it. I have to make a little trip to Mississippi and can pick you up. You have to be willing to do the job I have for you, though. Have you ever danced? For men, I mean."

I falter. I could have guessed it would be a job like this, but I'm really not sure how to answer. *Time to woman up.*

"No, but my mom used to, and I know I could do it."

"Good. I can teach you the ropes. It's not hard, but you can't be scared, you got it?"

"No way, I'm cool. It's no problem." *I hope my voice isn't shaking like my hands are.*

Marcus starts explaining the details of the job to me. It's more graphic than I expect, and my stomach is churning. I wonder if my mom did all this stuff. Hearing this man I don't know say these things in reference to me is surreal. It doesn't seem like real life, and it's frightening. I can't let Marcus know how scared I am. *Just act like it's all normal to you, Tiana. You can do it, no big deal.*

"And make sure you're there and on time when I come to pick you up. Don't back out on me, got it? I'll take care of you if you take care of me."

A couple of days later, in the evening, a black Lincoln Town Car pulls up in front of my aunt's place. I'm waiting outside. *Don't freak out until you know what's going on.* A big, well-dressed black guy gets out of the car and walks toward me. He's wearing designer jeans and a dark purple button-up shirt. He's very handsome.

"You're Tiana?"

I nod, and he asks, "Where's your stuff?"

"This is it. Just me and the clothes I'm wearing."

"All right, well, we'll fix that soon enough. Get in the car."

There's a skinny black girl in the car. She looks younger than me, maybe fourteen. She doesn't look at me and doesn't say a word. We drive for a little while, then stop at a pretty nice hotel and get two rooms. We're only about twenty minutes away from where I grew up with Grandma. Marcus puts the other girl in a room, and then he turns to me.

"Are you hungry?"

I nod.

"Come on." He takes me to the IHOP next to the hotel.

There aren't many people inside, and we sit in a booth in the corner. He starts asking me questions.

"Tell me about yourself. Where are your parents?"

"Well, my mom doesn't live too far from here, actually. But she's crazy and on drugs and stuff. My dad left when I was a baby, so I never knew him."

He asks more questions, and I tell him all about Grandma and my life with her, how I used to make good grades. I tell him about how my mom and all her siblings were abused by their dad and how they're all just messed up now. I even tell him my memories of my mom having sex with strangers. It's a little strange to me that Marcus is interested enough to listen, but it's so nice to be with someone who seems to care, I just keep talking.

I don't know what I expected Marcus to be like, but I didn't expect the man in front of me. With everything he does—the way he walks, the way he talks—he's so sure of himself and sounds educated. He flirts with the waitress, and we get a free pot of coffee. As he talks to me, I feel safe, like he really is going to take care of me. After being on my own for so long, I rest in the feeling that maybe there's someone to look out for me now.

We go back to the hotel, and Marcus takes me into the room across the hall from where the other girl is. My legs start to go limp, and my stomach's full of butterflies. I don't know what's going to happen, but I have a feeling he's going to tell me more about the job he has for me, and I'm terrified.

"Take off your clothes." My stomach flip-flops, and I look at him to see if he's serious. He's serious. *Oh, my gosh. OK, I'm not gunna run, and I don't think I can tell this guy no. He said he'd take care of me. There's nothing else for you, Tiana.* I turn away and take them off.

"Turn around, let me see you."

My heart feels like it's going to beat my chest open. I turn. *Why am I doing this?* I ask myself. *Because you can't be a little girl forever. Because you don't have anyone else to help you, so you might as well do this now and get it over with.*

"You look scared," he says.

"I've never been naked in front of anyone but my grandma."

He laughs.

"You're shittin' me, right?"

I shake my head.

"You mean to tell me you've never had sex?"

"Yeah, I'm serious. I've never done anything like this. I've never done anything with anyone."

At that, he cracks up. "Well, I guess I'll be your first!"

I'm shaking so badly, I can hardly control my hands. He has me get on my knees and then shows me how to give him a blowjob. I feel like I could faint.

This is it—this is your life now. Grandma's gone, childhood is over; it's time to grow up.

Then it's over. I'm relieved I don't have to do more. He stands over me.

"You should have gotten money for that, and every time you do it after this, it won't be for free. You got that?"

I nod, curled up on the bed with my eyes closed so I don't cry in front of him. I don't want to look at him, anyway. *Stop being such a little girl! How many of your friends were doing this and more with boys a long time ago? It's no big deal. Grow up!*

Marcus starts to leave, then turns around, walks over, and takes my face in his hands. I look up at him, and he says, "I guess like momma, like daughter, huh? Don't you ever forget what you came from."

I don't see him again until morning.

The other girl who was traveling with us gets dropped off at a house somewhere just outside of Atlanta. I never see her again. When we finally get into the city, we stay in a nice Comfort Inn in an upscale neighborhood. Alexis is there, with a few other girls, and we all have our own rooms. I get the feeling that none of them really like me. They're all very cold toward me, all except Alexis, who is her friendly self. But she goes straight to her room after I get there, so I spend some time resting in mine. I wake up to knocking at my door.

"Open up. It's time to get ready for work." It's Marcus.

I let him in, and he's holding a skimpy red dress. He tells me to take my clothes off and get on the bed. Then he starts getting undressed, and I know what's about to happen. He doesn't yell or force me. He doesn't have to. I'm so nervous I'm shaking, but I've made my decision. I'm in this for good and just have to suck it up and survive.

After he has sex with me, I put on the dress and attempt to do my own hair and makeup. One of his girls named Rochelle comes to my door. She has a black eye. "You're riding with me tonight. You follow my lead and do what I say. You don't, and you could end up in jail or dead behind a Dumpster, got it?"

I nod.

"Here's what's gunna happen: When a trick comes over, I do the talking. I make the deals, and when I tell you to go with him, you do whatever he asks. Don't look at anyone but the trick, and don't ever, *ever* come back without the full amount of money I set in the deal."

I examine her black eye and nod again.

She drives a black Mercedes to a shady looking part of the city, to a street called Forsyth. We just drive, windows down, back and forth on that street. Rochelle honks at the other cars driving by and motions for them to pull over. If they like what they see—either her or me—she makes a deal with them. They get back in their car, and we follow them, sometimes behind an old, run-down building and sometimes to one of the nasty motels nearby.

Everyone driving the street is here for the same thing; they're all either prostitutes or johns, and they're all in cars. No one is walking the streets; it's just driving and honking. Rochelle and I do this all night. I sleep with so many guys that night it doesn't seem real.

The first week is pretty crazy. I get arrested. I don't know what I'm doing yet; I just know I'm supposed to ask every guy I see if they want a date. I'm driving Forsyth, doing just that and, unaware, I ask a cop.

Honk! Honk! I wave out my window at a little Ford. This guy looks interested. I pull up next to him.

"Hey, handsome, wanna take me on a date?"*

He holds up a badge. "Pull your vehicle over, ma'am."

So I go to jail and sit there for three days until Marcus finally gets me out. When we get home, he punches me hard in the stomach. "That's for making me waste my time and money."

After that, I get arrested so many times it just seems like part of my routine. More than just going to jail, I'm ticketed regularly for solicitation. The local vice cops know me by name.

Clearly, this is not the dancing that Marcus led me to believe I'd be doing, but I'm not completely naive. A guy isn't going to offer to take care of you if all you're doing for him is dancing. And I'm going to do whatever I need to do to survive. This is my only choice, so I adapt quickly.

It's not long before Alexis leaves to go with another pimp, and I hardly see her after that. Eventually, Marcus moves all of us into a huge house in an upper-middle-class area of Atlanta. It's big enough for each of us to have our own room, and mine has a big, comfy bed and a closet full of clothes.

My days consist of sleeping as much as I can, waking up to Marcus banging on my door to get me up, then out driving the streets until morning the next day. The only break in my schedule is when I make the occasional trip to Walmart to buy condoms and other necessities. Marcus always makes sure his girls have everything they need as far as food, clothes,

---

* Date or trick: A term used to refer to a john or the activity of prostitution—for example, "with a date," "with a trick," "dating," "tricking."

and a comfortable place to stay, so I figure it's a pretty even exchange when I give him the money I've made after a long night of working.

Even though it's physically wearing doing this seven days a week, I'd rather have this than no roof over my head. I'm so tired all the time. Sometimes I fall asleep in the bathtub after getting home and don't wake up until Marcus is practically beating down the door. Mindlessly, I will my body to move and begin the routine that has become so familiar.

Marcus always makes sure I'm on time. Time is money, and we can't be one minute late to the job. He keeps all his girls in line with his rules: Don't be late, don't get drunk, and drugs will not be tolerated—at all.

One night, we're all getting ready, and down the hallway I hear Marcus shouting.

"You're wasting *my* time and *my* money! You knew the consequences when you bought the drugs."

I step out of my room and see clothes and things being tossed out the doorway of one of the rooms.

"Please, it was just this once, I swear! I've never even... "

"Stupid bitch, you were warned. You think you can use my money to feed your addiction? Get *out*. Now! Before I beat you!"

After that, I know Marcus is serious about his rules. The bottom line for Marcus is, it's all about the bottom line—the classier and cleaner the girl, the more money she'll bring in.

He doesn't even allow us to cuss around him because he says a real lady doesn't use those words. He even encourages us to use condoms—except, of course, when we sleep with him. I definitely don't need to complicate things with a pregnancy or STD.

The first time I have a condom break on me, I flip out. I'm with a john who looks real sleazy. Who knows how many girls he has slept with?

"Oh my god...oh my god! It broke—the condom broke! What do I do?" *This guy could have AIDS, for all I know. I could die because a freakin' condom broke!*

"Calm down, baby. It's not the end of the world. I shouldn't have even used one," he says.

"Just give me my money. I have to get out of here."

I rush myself to the ER. "I got raped. I need you to do a rape kit on me!" I lie to the lady behind the counter. She looks suspicious but says, "OK, I'll need you to fill out this paperwork."

Everything comes back fine—no STDs, no AIDS. I'm so relieved, I almost cry. After that, any time a condom breaks or I'm raped, I leave the job to go to the ER. I'm constantly paranoid that I'll get AIDS and die. Marcus will be so furious—probably beat me—if he ever finds out that I go to the hospital. Not only is he missing out on clients and money, but it means I am putting him at risk for getting caught and the authorities finding out that he's pimping me out. Of course, I never tell him when I go, but I'm more afraid of getting AIDS than I am of him.

I make sure I never go to the same hospital twice in a row, but there are only a few hospitals around Atlanta. As often as I have a scare, I'm in the hospitals enough that the nurses and doctors start to recognize me. I'd never tell them that I'm a prostitute, but they probably suspect it. All I say is that I've been raped and need them to do a rape kit on me. It's a messed-up thing to do, I know, but what other options do I have?

I learn a lot about how to look out for myself. Sometimes that means taking a lesson from Marcus about what happens when I don't follow his rules—such as not looking at a man who is not a trick.* One day, Marcus

---

* Reckless eyeballing: When a girl is engaged in eye contact too long with another pimp or male counterpart and appears interested in his appearance, car, clothes, girls, etc.

and a couple of us girls are walking down the street, and I look up at a man passing by me. Immediately, Marcus grabs my neck and pushes me around the nearest corner.

"You think I didn't see that, bitch?!" He hits me hard across the face. "Don't you ever, *ever* look at a man you aren't planning on fucking, you got that? You get off the sidewalk and walk in the street before you walk past another man!" He hits me one more time, and my nose is bleeding.

He doesn't always beat me, but after a while I've been hit enough that I almost get used to it. Somehow, I just turn off my emotions to everything. Things such as getting beaten or being raped by johns are just a part of my "normal."

One night, I'm in the car waiting for another girl, Kiki, to finish at a hotel with a john. A Hispanic man comes up to my window speaking Spanish. I understand enough to know that he's asking for directions. I barely crack the window to tell him, "Hablo muy poquito español" because I speak and understand only a little Spanish. I hear my passenger-side door open, and before I can even fully turn to see if it's Kiki, I'm punched in the face and dragged from the car.

The guy and his friend, who he's calling "cousin" in Spanish, throw me into the backseat of my car. They get in the front and start driving. We go for a few minutes and stop behind a building I'm not familiar with. The first guy gets in the backseat and rapes me. The other guy is up front waiting his turn. When the first guy is done with me, he says something to the other that starts an argument. I'm not exactly sure what they are saying, but I pick up enough to piece together something about shoving me in the trunk and taking me to someone's house. They try to fistfight between the seats and end up getting out of the car to fight. As soon as the door shuts, I jump into the front seat and take off. I can't believe they left the keys in the ignition. It's a miracle that I get away.

It's less than a month later, and my car breaks down at a 7-Eleven. I'm with another girl, Jocelyn. I see a good-looking, middle-aged white guy watching us as we open the hood, and he comes over.

"I can give you ladies a ride, if you need one."

"OK, sure, we don't have far to go," I say, and we get in his car.

As soon as we're in, he looks at Jocelyn and says, "I'd like to have a little fun with you before I drop you off."

"Sure, baby, whatever you want," she says, cozying up to him. She knows how to get the most money for her work.

He takes us behind a row of auto-repair garages.

"Yeah, it's safe here. I come here all the time," he says as though he's answering someone. He's talking fast, and I notice he has a wild look in his eyes. I realize he must be on something.

I get out of the backseat to wait outside, and *bam*! He's suddenly on top of me punching the shit out of me. I scream for help as I see Jocelyn disappearing around the corner of the garage. Like a switch being flipped, I feel myself shift—it's like my instincts kick in and the only thought in my head is *stay alive*. I fight back. I fight him as hard as I can, punching, kicking, screaming, 'til I think I'm going to pass out if he hits me one more time.

Then he grabs me by the hair and shoves me back in the car, down on the floorboard. Maybe he thinks all my screaming will attract attention, or maybe he thinks Jocelyn will come back with help. Whatever the reason, he drives me somewhere unfamiliar. He takes his hand off my head and lets me sit up. I go for the door, get out of the car, and begin running as fast as I can, but he's faster. He grabs me, throws me to the ground, and starts beating me. He starts taking sticks and anything he can use to rape me. It's a level of evil I've never experienced before. I know I'm going to die if I don't get away. I can feel his hatred for me and his desire to kill me. He takes out all his anger on my body. I'm starting to pass out, and he slaps me. "Don't you pass out on me, bitch!"

It feels like hours have gone by since I first got in this guy's car. He has to be on some strong drugs to be able to keep going the way he does. He beats me, then wears out. I try to run, and he catches me and beats me again. Eventually, I'm barely conscious, and I can tell he's finally losing strength. He sits down and pulls out a bag of crack and a pipe. He tries to get me to smoke with him, but I won't. He leans up against the building we're behind and inhales deeply.

I lie next to him on the concrete and watch fluid drip from his car parked in front of us. I'm too terrified to move, and my body aches so badly I don't even know if I can. I smell blood and urine. *Is it me or him?* I don't have the energy to look at myself to see.

He starts talking. *This guy is insane for sure.* He starts asking me questions like he wants to get to know me. Then the next minute he gets violent again and threatens me, saying he'll kill me if I tell anyone what he's done. I lie to him. I tell him I have a baby girl at home, and I just want to get home to her. I swear I won't tell anyone about him, and I don't even know who he is. I'm just a whore; cops don't listen to me anyway. I just want to get home to my baby, that's all I care about. I don't know if that's what makes him let me go, but he finally stands up, makes me give him all my clothes, walks to his car, and drives away.

I stay just a moment on the rough ground and watch his taillights disappear. *You have to get out of here, Tiana.* I don't know if I can sit up. *God, my body has never been in this much pain.* I force myself to sit and then start crawling. *That guy is crazy. What if he changes his mind and comes back. He could come back any second.* With that thought, fear and adrenaline surge through me, and I push myself up into a staggered run. I run into the first open business I see—an Asian karaoke bar. I'm crying and bleeding and completely naked. The workers there don't speak good English, but they wrap me in a blanket and hand me a phone. I call Marcus.

One day off to heal is all I get, and that's longer than Marcus wants to give me. He tells me that Jocelyn showed up at the house and told him what happened. She said she ran because the guy had a gun, which is a lie because I'm positive he would have pulled it on me if he'd had one. After going to the hospital and giving the authorities a description of the guy, I find out that he's a serial rapist and did the same thing to at least four other girls—all prostitutes. I figure this is just one of the dangers that come with the job.

After I've made it through my first year, Marcus comes to me and says, "I know it's been a little rough for you, but you had to pay your dues. I've got big plans for you, now that I know you can really hustle."

"What kind of plans?" He has me curious.

"There's a few new online connections I've made to get clients. We're going to use them to get you some upscale clients...men with real money. If you can do that, you won't have to drive the streets again."

"OK, but I don't understand. Why wasn't I with these 'upscale' clients in the first place?"

"Because I had to know you were right for the job. You had to prove to me that you're worth the investment I'm making in you. Now, I'll teach you how to speak like them, and how to carry yourself around them. These guys care about that kind of thing. They don't want a whore who looks and acts like one."

"What if I can't talk and act like them?" I don't know what a wealthy john would expect, but I don't think it'd be me.

Marcus slaps me across the face. "Look, bitch, stop with all the questions and complaints! You're going to do it! You'd better learn fast and appreciate what I'm doing for you. I'm the only person who cares enough to look out for you. If you'd had a dad to teach you this shit like a normal person, I wouldn't have to."

Marcus gets me hooked up with different Internet sites and several escort services run by women. I don't know where or how the women get their clients. They just call me and tell me a time and place to show up, and I do. It's totally different from when I was driving the streets. Marcus has me wear expensive clothing to go meet these clients, and it's always in a nice hotel. These johns will pay more for just a few hours than I made in several days when I first started out.

I would have guessed that these types of men would act like gentlemen—be less freaky and violent in bed than the johns I had dealt with on the streets. But they're just as bad, if not worse.

While I'm doing well, the rest of Marcus's business is not. Girls start leaving him. A few go with other pimps, and others go home, back to wherever they grew up. Marcus isn't like some pimps who force their girls to stay. He gives us the option of leaving, sometimes even lets girls come back. He might use physical force at times, but Marcus's main game isn't to just beat us into submission like some pimps do.* He charms and manipulates his way into our hearts, where he can do more than physical damage.** The thing is, I can't help feeling like I need him.

Eventually, I'm the only girl left. We move to a smaller place, and he and I share a room. We start hanging out, just to hang out, not for work. I used to hardly see him except when he came to wake me up in the evenings and then in the mornings to give him my money. I start thinking, *maybe he really cares about me, and we're going to be a couple.* But that doesn't last long. Sometimes we hang out with a pimp friend of his named Selfish. He

---

* Gorilla pimp: A pimp who uses violence as a primary means of control

** Finesse pimp: A pimp who uses psychological manipulation as a primary means of control

has a girl, Halo, who is to him what I am to Marcus. She and I get along; our friendship doesn't last long, though. Halo and I aren't ever allowed to hang out alone, without Marcus and Selfish there. Then one day Marcus tells me, "I don't want you hanging out with Halo anymore."

"What?! Why?"

"She's low class. I don't want you picking up bad habits from her. She could never get off the streets to do the kind of business we do. Selfish's OK with that, but I'm not OK with that for us, you understand? You owe me for what I've done for you, and I'm not going to let some cheap ho undo my hard work. If it wasn't for me, you'd still be on the streets whoring yourself out for pennies like your momma did."

"This is bullshit! She's the closest thing I have to a friend! And I'm fully capable of doing my job, thank… "

Marcus steps close to me, with a look in his eye that warns me not to cross him. "I said, it's over, you hear me, bitch?"

So I don't get to hang out with Halo anymore. And not long afterward, things start to really change. Marcus comes to me and tells me it's time to start rebuilding the business, and he needs my help.

"You're a smart girl, Tiana. Two people can get more accomplished than one, and I can teach you more about the business side of things. Nobody else is gunna do that for you. You're damaged goods, so who else would take you in? No one."

I know he's right. So he starts recruiting girls off the streets and from clubs, and I start training them.* A lot of the girls he gets are already

---

* Bottom bitch: A title of position for a girl who usually has been with the pimp the longest and consistently makes the most money. Responsibilities include running interference for and collecting money from the pimp's other girls, looking after the pimp's affairs while he is out of town or incarcerated, handling finances, and training and recruiting other prostitutes.

turning tricks for guys in clubs for extra money. They know exactly what they're getting into when they decide to go with Marcus.

He brings them in, and I coach them on driving Forsyth, how to deal with the police—everything. I'm the go-between from Marcus to the girls. Anytime a girl has a problem, she brings it to me, and if I need to bring it up with Marcus, I do. It's strange; in a twisted way, I feel like we're a boyfriend and girlfriend running a business.

Sometimes, a girl wants more time with Marcus—she feels like she is being ignored or that she could find a pimp who would give her more attention. Marcus tells me that as long as we have these other girls, I won't have to work as much. So even though it drives me crazy, I always tell Marcus when he needs to spend more time with one of the girls. I know it means he'll sleep with her and give her special attention, but I'd rather have to deal with that than taking more tricks.

One night, we've got about six girls out driving and Marcus gets a call from Selfish. Halo was out driving, doing her usual, and one of her regulars picked her up in his van. He beat her then choked her to death. I can't believe it. I've been choked plenty of times, and I know the feeling you get when you think you're about to die. But Halo really is dead. The reality sinks in that we're all just trying to survive.

Halo's death reinforces in me what I've known but haven't wanted to admit: Marcus isn't really my protector. My life is at risk every time I'm out with a john, and so are the other girls' lives.

But after Halo's death, life carries on as always. Sometimes we take road trips with the girls to other cities where we might be able to make more money. Marcus has connections with other pimps—he calls them "pimp partners." He calls these guys regularly to find out where they are, how they are doing, and what kind of money they're making. So, every now and then, we pick up and move for a month or two, following his partners to where the money is.

I hate going on road trips mostly because I hate traveling in cars. On road trips, we're packed in for hours—me, Marcus, and the girls.

Marcus decides to spend a month in Memphis, and I really hate it. Girls just walk the streets here, and it's worse to me than when I had to drive in Atlanta. In Atlanta, I at least had the protection of a vehicle when I was driving, but here I'm more exposed and vulnerable. In Atlanta, I can meet a client for drinks and no one else would know what I'm really there for. Here, it doesn't matter how expensive my clothes are; I'm walking the streets, so everyone knows what I am.

Marcus makes me go out there every night, and every night I'm scared for my life. But then, after a week of this, I get picked up by this guy Randy, who's a professional DJ. I spend the whole night with him, and we do a lot of talking. I tell Randy how much I hate walking the streets here, and he tells me he wants to help me. He gives me $1,000 at the end of the night. After that, he picks me up every night the rest of the time I'm in Memphis, and every night he gives me $1,000.

For the short amount of time I spend with Randy, we get to know each other really well. I tell him some of the crazy things that have happened to me with the more violent johns, and he starts thinking that he's going to save me somehow—get me to stop hustling.

"I want you to use this money for yourself," he says to me one night, handing me the usual $1,000. This time it's not cash, though; it's a money order.

"You know I can't keep it for myself. It all goes to Marcus."

"No, see, that's why I made it a money order. You can hide this easier than cash."

"Why are you doing this?"

"Have you thought about what you're gunna do one day? Do you really think you can do this forever? You're gunna need money when you start a new life. Promise me you will use this for that."

"OK." I immediately realize Randy is one of those johns who thinks he's my "savior." I've had plenty of johns like him; they get some kind of twisted gratification out of acting like they're going to help get a girl off the streets. But I'm definitely not going to turn down Randy's money, and he gets me thinking. I can't keep this life up forever.

Once Marcus has enough girls, I don't have to go on the road trips anymore. Everyone won't fit in one vehicle, and he needs someone to stay home and oversee the other girls he doesn't take with him. He leaves the girls who make the most money at home with me, and he takes the girls who aren't making much to see if they'll do better in another city.

With my new position, I don't have to take any new johns at all. I keep my regulars, but my primary job is overseeing the girls. I keep them in line, see a regular once or twice a week, and other than that I'm pretty free to do what I want. But while Marcus gives me some freedom, he always reminds me who I am—that I'll never be anything but a whore, and he's the only one who'll ever take care of me.

Marcus and I still share a room, even though we stay in big houses in the suburbs with all the girls. He likes the big houses, always making sure the landscaping is immaculate and parking our expensive cars where neighbors can see them. I wonder what the neighbors think. They have to have an idea about what's going on—big, black guy in a white, upscale neighborhood with a bunch of young girls who leave the house only at night and return in the morning? No one ever questions if Marcus is pimping us out, but I'm surprised we don't get the cops called on us more.

One of the only times we do have the cops called on us is on my twentieth birthday. Marcus is out of town, and I decide to treat myself to a new gym membership with some of the birthday money he gave me. My phone rings, and it's him.

"Hey, I need you to go to the house. I'm expecting a package, and I need someone to answer the door when it gets there."

"I'm at the gym getting a membership. I'm not going back to the house right now."

"Bitch, you'd better do what I say. Go back to the house. You do not want to see me later if you don't get back there now."

"No. It's my birthday, and I'm gunna do what I wanna do."

I hang up. I've never talked to him like that, let alone hung up on him. There will be hell to pay later. But for now, I'm going to have a day to myself, and I'll worry about him when I have to.

I get out of my car in front of the house, and I see Marcus. I run for the house, but he's too quick for me. He's furious. He yanks my hair hard from behind. My head jerks backward, and I fall onto our perfectly mowed lawn. Marcus hits me like I'm a punching bag, yelling, "Stupid bitch! You'll do what I say, when I say!"

There's no way our neighbors can ignore this. I don't know how long we're out there, but Marcus doesn't let up screaming at me. Finally, he lets go long enough for me to make a run for the house. He's right behind me, but a police car pulls up.

"Get upstairs!" Marcus yells at me. "Hide yourself! You'd better not make a sound!"

I run upstairs to our bedroom and hide under the covers. I hear the cops downstairs; Marcus yells that they have no right to come in and no proof that he's done anything wrong. But they go through all the rooms and finally make it to my room. I guess hiding under blankets on a bed isn't the most brilliant hiding place because they immediately find me, bruised and bleeding.

"Did this man beat you, ma'am?"

I lie. "No, I fell down the stairs. I'm just resting."

They question me some more, but I don't give up Marcus. He's still my man, and I'll protect him. Ultimately, they take him away, but it's not on an assault charge. They take him away for having a bunch of outstanding tickets or something. He's in jail only a few days.

While he's in jail, and any other time Marcus is gone, I become an accountant of sorts. The girls bring me what they make each night, and I keep a notebook that shows every cent that goes out and every cent that comes in. It all has to add up when Marcus gets home, but sometimes I don't mind doing a little creative accounting. I'll take a little extra spending cash for us girls and just change the income amount to match what we've spent. We can have a little fun while Marcus is gone.

But there's always that one girl who thinks it's her job to tell Marcus everything that's going on. This one girl, Natasha, comes along who especially wants Marcus's approval. She's the kind of ho who will do whatever it takes to get in good with Marcus and steal my place.

One day, after Marcus returns from a trip, Natasha says, "Thanks so much for the extra money, Marcus. You're so generous."

"What are you talking about? What extra money?"

"Oh, you know, the extra money Ti gave all of us while you were gone. I just assumed you knew, since it's your money."

He turns to me, and I know a beating is coming.

I see his fist clench. He raises his arm, and I start to take a step back. He moves fast, and I feel him make contact with my left eye, then my stomach. I crouch over in pain, but he's not done. He punches me again, then grabs my neck and slams me against the wall. He's yelling at me, but I'm starting to pass out and can't hear him. My vision is getting blurry. I see his fist coming toward me again, and everything goes black.

Marcus beats me in front of the other girls to make an example of me. It's part of his way of keeping everyone in line. I'm not even upset when one of the girls squeals on me. I used to think the same way they do and tell Marcus every time I saw a girl do something outside of his rules. Now I know how he works and don't mind bending the rules a little, even if it sometimes means getting punched around.

It's not that I enjoy getting beaten up, but to me, that's not as bad as when Marcus purposely tells me about the other girls he's sleeping with. I know he does it just to hurt me. Sometimes, he'll bring them into our room and sleep with them right in front of me because he knows I hate it. I go crazy and start yelling at him, and then he beats me worse than when I lie about money. I can't help it, though—how am I supposed to keep my mouth shut when he's doing things like that? My stomach churns, and my heart burns, and I have to scream at him—he's all I have.

As awful as he can be to me, it's the times he takes care of me that keep me with him. I know that out of all his girls, I'm the one who's most special to him. I'm the one girl who can go out whenever I want. If I ask him for money to go shopping, he gives me $200 when another girl would only get $50. I'm the one who has been with him the longest. Still, I know my loyalty to him will never be enough to keep him to myself.

One road trip we take makes me realize this more than ever. We're in Tucson with a few girls, and as usual, Marcus and I have a room together. One morning, I slip out of our room to run to the corner store. When I get back, I find him in bed with Natasha. I charge at her.

"Get out of my room, you stupid bitch!" I grasp for her neck.

Wham! Marcus backhands me so hard that I slam against the wall.

"I hate you!" I scream at him. Natasha is yelling at me, but I'm not listening. Marcus screams back at me.

"Tiana, you'd better calm down! You touch her, and I'll make you wish you never walked in here!"

I know he means it, and I'm so furious, I just have to get out. I have to leave him, this place, everything.

"I'm done!" I storm out and hear him yelling behind me, but I know he can't follow me out because he's not dressed. I make it to the sidewalk outside when I hear him behind me. I start running. The next thing I know, I'm on the ground and in more pain than I've ever been in my life. I'm screaming, I'm blacking out, I don't know what's happening. I catch a glimpse of Marcus's face, and he looks scared.

When I wake up, I'm in a hospital room. Marcus is standing near my bed, and we're alone. He doesn't look scared anymore.

"I told you to calm down. But you had to go and freak out and run away. This is what you deserve."

"What happened?"

"I kicked you in the back, and you fell on the curb and broke your femur. Doctors say you were lucky because one of your arteries was close to being punctured. You could have bled to death if I hadn't brought you here right away. You owe me your life."

Once I'm out of the hospital, Marcus leaves me in a hotel room by myself to recover. I have a cast on for weeks and can't go anywhere. All I can do is order room service and watch soap operas. As if I'm not already going crazy enough, holed up for weeks, Marcus occasionally comes by with girls and has sex with them in front of me. It's his way of getting back at me for standing up to him. He thinks he can make me jealous enough to stay with him after all of this. He's right.

When we're finally back in Atlanta and he knows I'm not leaving like I said I would, he buys me a puppy. I think he actually feels guilty for beating me up and then leaving me alone in the hotel. He's too proud to say he's sorry, so he buys me things instead.

Then Natasha starts being more trouble to me than ever. She wants Marcus's attention more than any other girl I've dealt with. She constantly challenges my authority and tries to make me look bad to Marcus. He starts pulling away from me, and I can't stand it. After a while, he's sleeping with her more than anyone—more than me. And one day he comes to me and says, "Natasha's pregnant."

Something breaks inside me. All these years, all these girls, and she's the one who ends up pregnant with his baby? I feel like all the circumstances surrounding my relationship with Marcus—all the fights, the beatings, him sleeping with other girls—it has all led to this moment. I decide to leave. I've wanted to leave before, but my ties to him have been too strong. This has finally severed them.

I figure Natasha can take over. She can be the battered and abused girl who thinks she's special, but really isn't. I pack up my bags and head to my friend Alana's. She used to be with Marcus, and she's still ho'ing, but now she has a place with her boyfriend. They let me sleep on their couch for the next six months.

I start dancing in strip clubs, and I still see my regulars. I try to save up enough money to get a car and my own place. So many times, I think about going back to Marcus. It would be so much easier. He always took care of me. And I miss him.

I'm finally able to get a car and a little utility apartment. It's lonely, though. This guy, Darrell, starts coming around a lot and seems to really like me. We hang out almost every day, but I know he's just a rebound. I don't even consider him a legitimate boyfriend because I'm still turning tricks to make money. But his presence helps me cope with the loneliness and boredom. I still think about going back to Marcus and the life. The crazy hours and adrenaline rush of a constantly dangerous lifestyle have gotten in my blood. It's hard to explain, but normal life is hard to adjust to. I hold out, keep working, and don't let myself think about it too much.

I guess I'm not as careful with Darrell as I am with my clients, because one month, I miss my period. This is the first time I've been pregnant. It's so hard to believe that after all these years, all those times a condom broke or I was raped, *now* I'm pregnant! I had always wondered, in the back of my mind, if something was wrong with me and I couldn't have babies.

But here I am, pregnant, and I want to keep this baby. I'm a little nervous, but I couldn't have imagined how thrilled I would be to bring a new, innocent life into this world. Thinking about this unexpected future with my child fills me with hope for a new life. Darrell isn't interested in being a dad, but I don't care. I'm going to look after myself and my baby.

She's a beautiful baby girl, with the prettiest black curls. I name her Hope. Darrell leaves not long after Hope arrives, and I know it's time to get out of Atlanta. There are too many bad memories here, and I don't think I'll ever be able to make a new life for myself and Hope unless I leave my past behind.

Alabama still feels like home, and it seems like the best place for us to go. We move just a few towns away from where I grew up, and I get a job working in a dance club there. I'm not prostituting or turning tricks—just dancing. Other than prostituting, that's all I know to do.

Then, one morning, I'm leaving the dance club, and I have a voicemail from a friend. He says Marcus is dead. He got in a fight with another pimp, and the guy shot him in the head.

I'm shocked—devastated, even. For all the horrible things he did to me, I did love Marcus, and I probably always will. In the end, the lifestyle for which he had lived all those years became the enemy that killed him.

There's no going back for me now. Life isn't easy—I've got horrible credit from Marcus putting things in my name and not paying them off, I can't get a respectable job because I have prostitution charges on my record, and working nights has me worn out most of the time.

But I've got my Hope, and she's my reason to keep pushing through the daily struggle of living. I'm making plans for her, and even for myself to go back to school. Now, I have to learn how to live instead of just survive. And that's a lot harder than I ever thought it would be. Even though doing what's wrong is so much easier, I'm realizing that living means choosing to do what's right for me and my little girl.

TIANA'S VOICE

Prevention

The period after my grandma died was really the pivotal moment in my life when, if things had gone differently, I probably never would have been trafficked.

Anyone who has lost a friend, their home, or their family knows how vulnerable you are after a loss like that. I lost all of those things when I lost my grandma, and I was still just a teenager in high school. There was nowhere for me to go, and the help I did get from friends met temporary physical needs—not long-term emotional, mental, and physical needs that come after such a major life change.

At the time, I wasn't the kind of girl who even dated. But being in such a desperate and helpless position pushed me into situations and decisions I normally would have stayed away from. If someone from my family, my school, or one of my friends' parents had reached out to help me, my story might have been different.

Maintaining Freedom

My record holds me back in a lot of ways. I have charges for public nudity and solicitation; financially, my credit is terrible because of all the things Marcus put in my name. It makes it hard to get a job and made it really difficult to go back to school.

I did get my GED and tried to go back to school to become a registered nurse. Education was always important to me, and although I've had to leave nursing school for now because of difficulties with work and raising a child, I'm proud to have achieved my GED. It's as good to me as the high school diploma I tried so hard to stay in school to get.

It has been extremely difficult staying positive. Depression and flashbacks hit me hard sometimes, and I don't always know how to deal with them. I've had to take care of myself for so long that it has been hard to trust or rely on other people for help. I'm considering going to counseling and have tried a couple of support groups, which I liked. It's difficult to stay committed, though, because I already work so much that I don't get much time with my daughter.

Words to the Wise

Something I would say to any kid or teenager who is in a situation similar to what I was in is to stay in school. I know that's not easy to do, but do everything you can to graduate. Go to your school counselor, nurse, teacher, or other safe adult and be open about your home situation. There are programs and people who can help.

Also, don't get caught up in anything that claims to earn you "fast money." Any job opportunity that promises a quick buck is probably a scam. I didn't know of any other way to make money, so I took a job dancing. It wasn't glamorous, fun, or sexy—it was hard and lonely, and it led me into a life of being prostituted. Don't be fooled like I was. I thought I was in control. I thought I was making my own choice, but really, I was being used. I was young, vulnerable, and easy to manipulate—just what Marcus was looking for. Don't be fooled and don't be silent. Tell as many adults as you need to until someone helps.

A large number of children have been raised in homes where exchanging sex for money or goods is a normal part of the family culture.

Chapter 4

FAMILIAL TRAFFICKING

"My mother was my first pimp. She used to sell me to the landlord and other men who wanted a young girl. She was a junkie.... I thought that was normal."

—A survivor[1]

IN THIS DAY AND age, we would not be surprised to hear that some children suffer incest and sexual abuse in their own homes. Not so acknowledged, however, is the rise in sexual abuse coupled with child sex trafficking within families.

All In The Family

Many children fall victim to being sold by their own family members in exchange for cash, drugs, to pay off debt, or even for food. Such is the story of five-year-old Shaniya Davis, who was sold by her mother into sexual slavery as payment for a two-hundred-dollar debt. Six days after being sold, her body was

Photo: Antoinette Davis. City of Fayetteville Police Department

found in a nearby field. An autopsy determined that she had been sexually assaulted and suffocated.[2]

> *"I have a friend who, as a very young child, was frequently asked by her father to 'spend time' with one of his buddies in the neighborhood. After the molestations, the abuser would always provide this girl's father with a big meal. This child was being trafficked in exchange for a steak dinner!"*
>
> —Alisa Jordheim, founder, Justice Society

A large number of trafficked children have been raised in homes where exchanging sex for money or goods is a normal part of the family culture. Because many of these children are indoctrinated into sexual exploitation at very young ages, they do not recognize having sex with adults as abnormal behavior.

> *"A fourteen-year-old girl suspected of prostitution told police her mother and grandmother, both convicted prostitutes, forced her to sell her body to pay their living expenses."*[3]

Why Don't They Leave?

When a controlling member of a family is the trafficker, it can be difficult for a child to leave the home or report the abuse. Fear and shame are two primary silencers that stop children from seeking help. In some cases, family members will guilt the child into a sense of duty to provide income and support the family. In other cases, a child may be threatened with violence or death against herself or other family members. Emotional attachments to younger siblings can create fear in a child that if she leaves, her siblings will be forced into trafficking in her stead.

"I have been pimped all my life, used by my family, and sold to any Johnny-come-lately.... I wanted to run every day, but what would I do with a sixth-grade education and make the money I was making, and who is to say they would let me walk like that?"

—Chicago ex-pimp[4]

As is common in sexual abuse cases, many children fear that reporting the crime will either break up the family, or provoke anger or repercussions from other family members. The trafficker may also convince the child that she has willingly engaged in prostitution and will be arrested if she reports the activity.[5]

"Although most adolescents reported telling an adult about the abuse, more than 75 percent of these adults were not concerned or supportive about their situation."[6]

Victims Are Hard To Identify

Children who endure commercial sexual exploitation frequently fall through the cracks of our social system. They are commonly misidentified by frontline workers, including emergency room staff, teachers, and counselors. Law enforcement officers have the particularly challenging task of identifying whether a victim is an adult or a minor. To complicate matters, many traffickers will provide girls with false identification and instruct them to say they are older than eighteen.[7] When interviewed by law enforcement, girls are often unwilling or unable to identify as victims. They also can be difficult and evasive due to their distrust of authority figures. This misidentification by adults and distrust from the girls creates a chasm that hampers many youth from getting the help they need.

"When youth are approached by traffickers, pimps, exploiters, they don't see much difference between their purpose of bringing finances into their foster home and bringing money to traffickers, pimps, exploiters' stable...." [8]

—Child survivor

While familial trafficking is not new, the recognition and reporting of this crime is still in developmental stages. Shared Hope International's 2009 National Report on Domestic Minor Sex Trafficking reported, "Trafficking of children by family members was noted frequently in the assessments done by Shared Hope International. Due to a lack of training and understanding of human trafficking by state child protection service agencies, professionals often classified the abuse under a different label, such as child sexual abuse. This mislabeling of child sexual abuse instead of child sex trafficking results in the commercial component of the crime being lost." [9]

Slowly, but surely, the tide is changing, and recognition of this crime is growing. Many states are now passing legislation requiring child sex trafficking awareness training for all frontline workers, including law enforcement agencies, public schools, and child care services. Additionally, Senate Bill S.1118—Child Sex Trafficking Data and Response Act of 2013, introduced in June 2013, would require that foster care and adoption assistance agencies officially document any child who has been identified as a victim of sex trafficking. [10] Legislation is a good first step, but it's not enough in itself. We must be diligent to ensure that that once laws are passed, they are effectively put into action.

There Is Hope

"'I actually can go to college now!' One of our twelve-year-olds shrieked after spending four days struggling and fighting over not understanding

negative numbers. Days ago, not only had she given up on learning the concept, but her frustration led her to believe she was stupid and that she should just run away and go back to the life because she didn't feel she was good at anything else. The joy that erupted from her after doing ten problems correct went so much deeper than a grade on a paper. It allowed her to hope in a future again—a future separate from slavery. She is now fourteen years old and on track with her education!"

—Melissa Hermann, executive director, Courage House

The Inside Story

You are about to read Kate's story of being trafficked by her own family. After eight years of captivity, 2013 was a landmark year for Kate. She was officially out of the "life" longer than she was in it—2013 began her ninth year of freedom. We rejoice with Kate for the milestone!

LOSING KATE:
FROM INNOCENCE TO INFAMY
By K. D. Roche

It has been almost a year since we moved from Oregon to Colorado. Once Mom quit using drugs, Dad didn't come to visit anymore, so she didn't see any reason for us to stay. We moved, and she found a boyfriend pretty quickly. She didn't seem to mind fulfilling the promise she made to my grandparents that she would send me back to Oregon every summer to spend time with Dad's family. She probably wanted time alone with her boyfriend anyway. Now the year has passed, and I am finally going back to visit.

Butterflies stir in my stomach as I board the plane to visit Grandma's. It's my first time flying alone. I feel grown-up and responsible, and a little nervous. Not many seven-year-olds fly by themselves. I straighten to appear as tall as possible. The two-and-a-half-hour flight seems like only five minutes as daydreams of summer fast-forward me to Oregon.

My eyes search the crowded waiting room for Grandma—a tall, slender woman with kind eyes. I spot her waving and run to greet her. I miss seeing her often like I used to. We walk to the parking garage. My cousin, Joe, waits in the car. As soon as I open the door, he springs over the backseat, wrapping his arms around my neck in an excited hug. He's the same age as me, but he has always been shorter and smaller. We laugh and sing on the hour-long drive home from the airport.

The dogs greet us with happy barks, and Aunt Lisa and Uncle George spread open their arms for hugs. Aunt Lisa seems so much happier since she married Uncle George two years ago. I had never met any of her previous husbands, just Joe's real dad and Uncle George, but the family says they like Uncle George best. They say he's a hard worker. I like him better, too. He's a lot nicer than Joe's dad. Joe's dad always yelled at us and hardly came home, but neither Joe nor I have seen him since he and Aunt Lisa got divorced. Uncle George is different. He gives us ice cream and lets us watch movies. If we do something wrong, he doesn't yell; he just helps us get it right the next time. Joe even calls him "Dad" sometimes.

Summer is here, and the family is finally together. In a few days, I could be riding horses with Aunt Lisa. *Maybe she will let me ride her horse again while she trains new colts,* I think. *She trusts me with the horses. It's one thing I know I can do right. At home, I never do anything right. Every day, Mom's boyfriend yells at me for something. Mom doesn't like it when he yells, but she never does anything to stop it.* I imagine the wind blowing on my face as I ride along the pasture. It feels so free. I feel so confident and in control when the reins are in my hands and my feet in the stirrups.

After dinner, Grandpa makes a bed on the floor for us kids to sleep on. He always sets us up in the living room so we can fall asleep watching movies.

Seven. The age of Popsicles. The age of slumber parties. The age of innocence.

Everyone is asleep, but *Lion King* isn't over yet. I roll over and feel a hairy arm touch mine. My eyes want to open, but fear demands that they remain closed. *Who is lying next to me?*

I yawn and readjust, hoping to deter the hand that grazes me intrusively. I pretend like I am waking. Uncle George smiles at me.

"I need to go to the bathroom." I get up, walk to the bathroom, and close the door behind me, but the doorknob turns and the door pushes open.

"Shhhh," he says, "everyone is sleeping."

He closes the door behind him and turns the lock. I don't speak, but I am screaming loudly inside. No words escape my mouth, only tears from my eyes. His hands invade my body, but his actions trespass my soul. There is blood on my clothes—stains that will be tossed and forgotten. There is pain and fear—memories that forever stain the paradigm in which I view the world.

"You don't want anyone to know what a naughty girl you are. If they know what *you* did, they'll be disgusted with you. Better you don't say a word, unless you want to be punished." He grabs me, and I jerk away from him. He laughs. "This isn't even the beginning, little girl. Now stop actin' like you didn't ask for it. You think you can just sleep on the floor right in front of me? You think I've been playin' games with you, buyin' you toys and candy, expectin' nothing from you in return? Grow up! You wanted me. You *still* want me."

I don't understand. What did I do wrong? What did I say to him? Did I want it? NO! I never said...but I did ask him to play games with me. I did ask him to buy me candy.

"Shhhh," he says, "shhhhh. Everyone is sleeping."

My soul slept that night. In fact, it hibernated for the next nine years.

Nine. The age of fear. The age of silence. The age of obedience.

I step off of the plane and hug Grandma, breathing in the familiar scent of her homemade laundry detergent. I can't wait to see my cousins. I hope Uncle George won't be there when we arrive. The dogs bark, running in circles. The pitter-patter of their little paws prancing on the tile welcomes us in as we arrive. Aunt Lisa and Uncle George stand up from the couch, stretching out their arms. Uncle George whispers in my ear as he leans in for a hug, "Don't you worry, hun, we've got all kinds of plans for you kids this summer." My stomach turns as I swallow the memories of the years before.

"Joe!" I run to greet him. He looks the same—tiny build and straight blond hair. He stares at me. I hug him with both arms, but his body is stiff. *Something is not right.*

Grandpa makes us a bed on the floor in the living room, as he always does. I ask him if I can have my own sleeping bag. *A Bug's Life* is playing, and Joe and I are still awake. Everyone else is asleep. Everyone—except for Uncle George. He walks into the living room and waves for Joe and me to follow him. *He wants both of us? Has he touched Joe before, too?* I really don't want to go with him, but I am afraid to refuse. We follow him into the office, and he closes the door. I clench my eyelids tightly and hold my breath. My ears feel plugged up as I try to brace myself for what I know is coming.

I wait.

For my clothes to be discarded. For the intrusive hand.

One one-thousand. Two one-thousand... ten one-thousand.

I open my eyes.

Uncle George is sitting in the computer chair, next to Joe.

"You know where you are going?" he asks.

"Got it," says Joe.

"Good. You've been working with me almost two years now, and I expect you to remember what I taught you. Stay in control and give them exactly what they want."

I watch silently, relieved he hasn't touched me. *What does he mean "give them exactly what they want?" Who? What has Joe been doing working with Uncle George? I thought Uncle George was a ranch hand and Aunt Lisa has been home-schooling Joe.*

He closed the door, so it is coming. It has to be coming.

"We're going to teach you a game." Uncle George says with a smile. "All you have to do is exactly what we tell you, and there won't be any problems." *We? So Joe is in on this now, too?*

Joe maneuvers the mouse, typing various things into the computer. The screen pops up. "Teen Chatroom." Joe creates the name "2young4u." Immediately, the computer screen is filled with five or six pop-up chats.

"Hey, baby, age/sex/location?"

"9, female, Oregon."

"Is 45 too old?"

"45 is perfect."

He's obviously done this before. He responds to the messages robotically, without thought.

"How young?"

"9 too young?" Joe responds.

"Is 55 too old?"

"55 is perfect."

"Do you have pictures?"

"I can take some."

Uncle George is smiling. "OK, kiddo, we're going to take some pictures." First he snaps a couple of me just standing there. "Smile," he says. A tear forms in my left eye. I wipe it away before he notices. He takes pictures of me in my T-shirt and underwear, in all sorts of sitting and standing positions.

Joe is still typing away at the computer. "All right, George, they want the pictures."

"All right, honey, you can put your clothes back on now."

He has pictures. What is he going to do with my pictures? Why did he make me do those things?

Uncle George removes the memory card from the camera and inserts it into the computer. I stand behind my cousin and read the multiple chats on the computer screen. "Can I see a picture?" one person asks.

"Sure," Joe types, "as long as you are sure you don't mind that I'm only 9."

"I don't mind. I like it."

Joe e-mails a picture of me to this stranger. "Can I go to the bathroom?" I ask, hoping to escape the room, even if only for a moment.

"No. I want you to read everything Joe types. You need to learn how to do this."

The stranger asks, "Have you ever had sex before?"

Joe types, "Yes."

"And you liked it?"

"I liked it," Joe types.

"Mmm, bad girl!" the stranger replies.

The words Joe types cause the anxiety in my belly to rise up into my throat. I can feel more tears coming, but I won't release them. I can't let them know how I feel. *I remember the first time. It was here. In that bathroom. I didn't like it. I hated it. I still hate it. I hate that bathroom. I hate Uncle George. I hate this room. I hate those pictures. I hate myself.*

"Send me more pictures. Less clothes this time."

Joe sends the pictures.

I don't sleep all night. Instead, I am forced to stay awake reading messages in a chat room. Messages that make me feel dirty. Messages that make me feel like an object. Messages that make me feel ashamed. Messages from me. Dirty words. Dirty pictures. I am a dirty girl. Joe's words masquerade as my words. He types in my place, offering my body to the strangers he encounters online. They think they are communicating with me, but my cousin is actually the one chatting.

"Are you alone?" a stranger asks.

"No," Joe types, "My cousin is here, too."

"Boy or girl?"

"Boy."

"How old is he?"

"He's nine, too."

"I want you to have sex with him, and take pictures. Send them to me," says the stranger.

Joe looks at Uncle George, who says, "Do it. I'll type."

"Please, don't make me do this," I beg. Uncle George turns around in his chair and slaps me across the face. Everything in my face feels numb. I wish my whole body felt numb.

My body hurts. I can't think anymore. All I want to do is sleep. Uncle George throws me a wet washcloth. "Here," he says, "Clean yourself with this." He sends the pictures to the stranger.

"Who took these?" the stranger asks.

"My uncle did."

"Really? He's OK with it? Do you have sex with him, too?"

"Yes."

"You should have sex with him, too. Record it and take pictures. I want to see it."

Uncle George always does what the men in the chat room want. When they want pictures, he takes them; videos, he shoots them. I don't even know how I feel anymore. I feel how he tells me to feel. I do what he tells me to do. I can't think for myself, act for myself, or even dress myself anymore. I have lost myself to a role that I didn't audition for.

The next night is the same. Joe types. Uncle George watches, delegating if necessary. Uncle George starts calling me "slave." He doesn't call me "honey" or by my name anymore, just "slave." Joe calls me "slave," too. It's like he doesn't know me anymore. He acts as if we were never close. He looks at me with disgust and talks to me like I'm a bad dog. *What happened? I used to have fun with Joe. We laughed together and played games. He stood up for me when I got made fun of and made me feel special. Something is wrong with him now, and it scares me.*

I get in the shower, turning the knob almost all the way to hot. I scrub my body vigorously with the rough side of a sponge. *Maybe if I scrub hard enough, I will feel clean again.*

I sit in the corner on the bathroom floor and cry. *I still feel dirty; nothing makes me feel clean.* My skin stings, my body is sore, and my mind is numb.

I wake up early and sneak outside to call Mom. We don't normally talk much while I'm visiting Oregon. She figures no news is good news, and I figure that there's not a whole lot to say. Sometimes she will call to ask Grandma if everything is going OK, but we don't usually talk to each other. She answers the phone. "Hello?"

"Hey Mom, it's me, Kate."

"Hi honey. Is everything OK?" As soon as the words come out of her mouth, I can't speak. I try to form words, but only sobs come out. "What's wrong, baby?"

"It's Joe. And Uncle George. They keep making me do things I don't want to do."

"That's just part of growing up, baby."

"No, Mom. I mean bad things. Dirty things."

"I know what you're talking about. I read your journal last summer."

"What?"

"I read everything. I wasn't going to embarrass you by saying anything. After you came home from Oregon, you left your journal open on your desk in your room. I read what happened. You are just getting older. Men can't help themselves; they're curious. Your Uncle George didn't mean any harm by what he did. Joe's getting older, too, so I'm not surprised now that he's giving you a little attention. His hormones are probably just a little crazy. It's a normal part of growing up, honey. Boys are sexual. It only gets worse as they get older. You'll be OK. It'll help you to grow up a little. But listen, I have to go. Don't worry so much. Try to go with it. It makes everything easier and more enjoyable. I'll see you in August!"

She read my journal? How could she know this was happening and not say anything? Why would she make me come out here to visit if she knew? Normal? Did this happen to her, too? I don't understand. Is my whole life going to be like this? I don't think I can do this. Suddenly, I feel dizzy. My stomach tightens, and I bend over, getting sick all over the flower beds.

"What are you doing out here?" Uncle George yells, startling me to a standing position. I stand in front of the phone, hoping he won't see it.

"I felt sick, so I came out to get some fresh air."

"Get inside. Now!"

Grandma is sitting in her recliner in the living room. "Are you OK, sweetie? You look a little pale. You're too thin. You know, if you don't stay healthy, you won't be able to do the things you love, like riding horses with your Aunt Lisa. Sit down. I'll fix you something to eat."

I don't want anything to eat. I'm sick.

"Mom, I don't want to go to Oregon this year. Please don't make me go. Can't I stay home?"

"Sweetie, that's ridiculous. You have to spend time with your dad's side of the family, and you love riding horses with your Aunt Lisa. This is the only time you see them besides the three weeks you spend there for Christmas vacation."

"I don't want to go." *I do want to ride horses, but not if it means staying in the same house as Uncle George and Joe.*

"Well, you're going. And you'll have a great time."

My nerves keep my stomach in constant distress. I throw up every day for at least a week before leaving. I don't eat. I can't eat. *Maybe if I don't eat, I'll starve. Then this will end.* I cry myself to sleep every night. I pray to die.

The summer of twelve is here.

The age of acceptance. The age of submission. The age of dissociation.

I board the plane. My body trembles involuntarily, and goose bumps rise on my arms and legs. The flight attendant asks me if I am all right. I nod my head, though part of me wants to ask her if it is possible for me to get off of the plane. As the plane takes off, my anxiety bubbles like a volcano from the base of my stomach, until the little bit of breakfast I managed to eat erupts from my mouth into the aisle. The people around me are holding their noses and gagging. *God, I am disgusting. They know I'm dirty.* No one wants me around. Just Uncle George. Just Joe.

When I arrive in Oregon, I don't see Grandma. I sit and wait for her. Large hands press down on my shoulders from behind. "You ready, little slave?" I feel the hot breath of his whisper in my ear. A chill goes through my body, and suddenly I am cold. I stand up.

"Daddy missed you," he says.

"Is this your dad?" the flight attendant asks me. I nod. *Why can't I just say no?*

We walk out to the parking garage. Joe is waiting by the car. He's taller than he was last year, but he's just as skinny, and he's still shorter than me. "You're gonna have lots of fun this summer, little slave," Uncle George says with a laugh. Joe looks back at me but doesn't say anything. His eyes seem crueler than the year before. He appears aloof. We drive for more than an hour before I realize that we aren't going to Grandma's house. "Where are we going?" I ask.

"We're going to the ranch house."

"Aren't we going to Grandma's for a few days first?"

"No," Uncle George says, "She's sick. Worse than she was before. Some days she can't remember who her own kids are. Bringing you to see her would just confuse her more. The doctors say she has Alzheimer's. It'll only get worse. She probably already forgot you." *Is she going to die? Will I ever get to see her again?* I try to forget the way things were. I know they'll never be the same. Staring out the window, I try to focus on the fields, the shops, the trees—anything but Grandma. Still, I cannot forget her gentle voice. "Honey, I love you," she told me every day. *I know she does.* She would tuck my little flyaway wisps of hair behind my ears. *She couldn't forget me. She wouldn't forget me. Would she?*

Uncle George stops at a convenience store and fills the truck with gas. When he gets back in the car, he throws me two ice cream sandwiches. "Eat these, little girl. Nobody wants to be with a scrawny woman."

We drive another hour or so. I keep hearing Uncle George's words. *Nobody wants to be with a scrawny woman.*

But I'm not a woman. I am twelve years old. And I don't want to be with anybody. I just want to be alone. I just want to see Grandma. I just want to disappear.

Uncle George takes my bags, and I never see them again. He walks me to the guest house. There's a twin bed with a sheet on it and a dresser with broken drawers. Inside the drawers are some clothes—thin, sheer material in red and black, and a cheerleader uniform. There is a box in the bottom drawer. In it is a pair of handcuffs and other items. The windows are broken, and the room is decorated with pictures of horses, cowboys, coiled ropes, and horseshoes. The carpet is dirty, and there are spiders and cobwebs along the corners. It smells musty and is cold.

"All right, you little cum-slut slave, we're going to have some fun with you. After today, you won't ever forget that you're a fucking whore. I want you to always remember what you are. Joe's going to be your master now. You call him 'Master.' Call him anything else, we'll beat the shit out of you. Got it?" I nod. "I'll be around, but when I'm not, Joe owns you." *Owns me?*

"And I sure as hell know you ain't gonna tell nobody about this. You get to talk when one of us tells you that you can talk. Any questions?"

I shake my head.

"Good. Now come with us. We are going to get something to eat. We have big plans for you later."

I stare down at the burger and fries in front of me. *I'm not hungry.* "I can't wait to see how this goes," Uncle George says to Joe. "I have a feeling we're going to be in business here real quick."

I push the fries around my plate with a fork. *Nobody wants to be with a scrawny woman.* Uncle George puts a twenty-dollar bill on the table, and we head to the truck.

"That's a nice horse trailer you got there, cowboy. I bet that cost you a pretty penny," a stranger remarks as Uncle George unlocks the truck.

"Yeah, it's real nice. Wasn't my check, though. The perks of being the main cowhand for a rich man."

"Must be nice." The dusty stranger looks over the trailer again.

"Like to take a look inside?"

"Sure would." They disappear and don't come out of the trailer for ten minutes or so. When they emerge from the trailer, the stranger gives Uncle George a hard pat on the shoulder and winks at me. "I'll be seeing you a little later, darlin'." My stomach churns, and I feel the urge to throw up. *I have to find a bathroom, quick. I've got to get rid of this nasty feeling in the pit of my stomach.*

Thirty minutes later, we pull in to the county fairgrounds. Trucks and trailers are parked everywhere. Horses are tied up to fence posts, and every available stall is full. Lawn chairs and coolers are set up all over the place. Everyone is wearing boots and buckles, and most men have a faded circle in their back pocket from where they keep their chew.

"Don't worry, slave. You'll get used to rodeo," Joe says. "People help each other out around here. Everybody's got a little something that somebody else has need of. You'll find that out real quick. Tradin' is an easier way of life."

Slave. The word triggers memories of everything Uncle George said: "I want you to always remember what you are." I remember the warnings he gave me. My heart beats rapidly, and I suddenly feel faint. It seems that every other man who passes by is looking me up and down, giving me a nod or a wink.

"Good god, bitch! Stop shaking!" Joe mumbles at me.

"Hey there, cowboy!"

"Hi, Pete." Joe shakes his hand. "You here to shoe the horses?"

"Yes, sir," he says with a wink. The way he is looking at me makes me feel like I need a shower.

Joe grabs my hand and walks me to the other side of the trailer. "Pete's going to shoe the horses, and when he's done, you are going to pay him."

"But I don't have any money." My eyes scan the area. I want to run but see nothing but dirt in every direction. *Where would I go?*

"You don't need any. You just let him take you into the trailer. There's a bed in there. You do whatever he tells you to do and act like you like it. You remember what you are now, don't you? You are a sex slave. Ain't nothing goin' to change about that. You are going to learn to like this. Understand?"

I couldn't think of anything to do but to cry out, "Joe!"

"Stop it. I am not Joe to you anymore. I am your master! Don't look at me like that. Just do it."

"What did he do to you?" I ask. "Uncle George is a monster! Did he rape you, too?"

Before I can react, Joe knocks me to the ground and spits on my face. "You say anything like that to me ever again and I'll beat you like the worthless piece of shit you are. Now get up off the ground, slave. I'm nothing like you. I'm the one in control here!"

Kicking the dirt, he walks over to the step that leads to the trailer door and takes a seat. His eyes don't stop watching me. I won't let him see me cry. I pick up a rock from the ground and throw it as hard as I can into the dust. For a half second, I feel better. I pick up another, chucking it as hard as I can. Adrenaline is pumping through my body. Hate and anger like I have never felt before form a burning sensation in my stomach. My mind is filled with violent thoughts and words I've never spoken aloud.

"He's ready for you." Joe grabs my arm and shoves me up the step. The door slams shut behind me. Twenty minutes pass. The farrier steps out of the horse trailer. I pick up my clothes from the floor. My body is stiff. One of the straps to my halter top is torn, and it no longer ties around my neck. I search the trailer and find a T-shirt in one of the drawers. I pull it over my head. Searching for a brush, I try to comb my matted hair with my fingers. Looking into the mirror, I don't recognize my own eyes.

The door swings open. It's Joe. "You have two minutes," he says. "Someone else is here to see you."

I could run or fight, but I don't have the energy. I have no idea where I would go. Home is so far away. I climb back on the bed, pull up the comforter and hide beneath the covers. I bury my head into a pillow. I close my eyes and wish I were dead. *God, where the hell are you? What have I done to deserve this?* The door swings open. A tall, slender man appears. His face and clothes are dirty, and he smells like horse manure. "What are you doin' under the blankets?" he snaps. "Didn't you know I was comin'? Get up outta there." He spits a mouthful of chew into an empty beer can that he picked up from the floor.

I pull down the covers a little and sit up. "How 'bout you hurry the hell up?" His red eyes are glaring at me, and his right hand yanks the covers off of the bed and onto the floor. "You ain't gonna give me no problems. I'll be sure o' that!" Knocking me on my back with his forearm, he puts his weight on my chest with his knee.

I can hardly breathe; his knee presses hard against my ribs. One hard swallow and my emotions are gone. I feel pressure against my body. His mouth moves. I know he is talking to me, but I can't hear what he is saying. I smell dirt, sweat, and tobacco. "Answer me, cunt!" His fist blows against my jaw. I taste blood. "You must make your family sick!" *I never thought about what they think of me. Mom doesn't care. Aunt Lisa never says anything. I'm just a whore now. Nobody really cares. Just Joe and Uncle George.*

"Thanks for nothin', bitch! I guess I'll be seein' more of you since I reckon your man is gonna be wanting more of this," he says, holding up a clear bag of white powder. *They did this for drugs? Am I gonna have to do this every time they need more drugs? Every time the horses need shoeing? Every time they can't pay for something?*

Rodeo days turn into rodeo weeks. We travel to many places. The names all blur together. Rodeo weeks become rodeo months. I stop keeping track of the days—it seems easier that way. I stop counting the people. "A lot" seems like a lot less than if I had to say an actual number. As the days and numbers grow longer and larger, I become further dissociated from reality. The only truth I know is that I cannot trust anyone. Every imaginable person passes through the door of the trailer. Young faces and gray beards. Cracked hands and painted fingernails. Business suits and cowboy boots. A county drug dealer and a county officer. At the end of each summer, I return to Colorado, each passing year with a little more hatred toward humanity and a lot less self-respect.

Uncle George drives down the farm road that leads to the ranch house, and I recognize where we are going. Aunt Lisa has a big meal prepared to welcome us home. Some of the people Uncle George works with are there, as well as some of the neighbors and their kids. Everyone gathers around picnic tables outside. They talk about their horses, cattle, and the weather. Kids are jumping into the pool with messy faces. The older kids are playing a game of hide-and-seek.

"Look at you," Aunt Lisa says, "You hardly look fifteen! You still have lots of growing to do!" *I've got no growing to do. I have zero plans on gaining a pound or starting to look any more like a woman. I wish she would leave me alone about the way I look!*

"Come on, Kate, I want to show you something!" Joe grabs me by the wrist and pulls me after him. We walk down the gravel road to one of the hay barns, where three older teenage boys are waiting inside.

"You've gotta be kidding me. I didn't know you were really serious!" one of the boys says. His eyes are wide, and his steps are shaky. He's smiling.

"All right, slave, do whatever they want. If you mess up, I'll know. I'll be watching." Joe whispers. I look over at the boys. The smallest of the three is much bigger than I am. He has long, unruly hair and looks very strong for his age. He looks about sixteen. The other two boys look older. Eighteen, maybe. I walk inside, and two of the three boys escort me farther into the barn. Joe waits outside.

When they leave, I am too weak to stand. Joe comes back inside the barn. "Get up!" he demands. "Come around the back with me. I'll take you to the bathroom and you can clean yourself up. You look like a ho. You don't want everyone to know how loose you are."

I turn on the shower and step in. The water pressure stings my skin. My tears are lost with the shower water, disappearing down the drain. I hear people talking and laughing outside of the door. The company is still here. I hear the boys from the barn. They are laughing about how scared I looked. *I hate them. I will never let anyone think I am scared ever again. I can handle them. I can do this. That's the last time I cry. I'm fine.* My body trembles. *They didn't hurt me.* I apply makeup to cover the bruises on my face, neck, and chest. *I don't care.* I dress myself in the clothes laid out for me on the counter. Laying my towel on the ground, I curl myself up on the floor and try to rest. I feel safer in the bathroom with the door locked.

My body jolts at the sound of banging on the door. "Kate, are you still in there? Open the door!" It's Aunt Lisa. I am relieved to hear her voice.

I've always been close to her, and I know I can tell her what happened. She won't listen to anything I say about Uncle George, since he is her husband, or Joe, since he is her son, but I know she cares more about me than those boys—they're not even family.

I crack the door slightly, giving her just enough room to slide in. "What is going on?" she asks. "Why are you in here? Have you been crying?" I remember my promise and refuse to cry, but I can't find my voice. "What's wrong, honey? You can talk to me."

"Those boys out there—Joe's friends. They raped me."

Her face looks stern. "Rape is a strong word. You shouldn't use that word. I'm sure that's not what happened. If you tell anyone about this, you could be taken from the ranch. You would never be able to ride horses again, and I know how much you would hate that. And you know the family would hate you if you said anything. It would ruin our family."

"I won't tell anyone. Just don't let them stay the night, please."

"I won't. But you have to come out of the bathroom."

She swore she wouldn't let them stay the night, but she let them anyway. *She didn't keep her promise, but I am keeping mine. They will not hurt me anymore. I'm through crying. I can do this.* I walk to the liquor cabinet and drink straight from the bottle of Jack. *I'll be fine.* I see the boys again. There are other guys there, too. This time, I give them exactly what they want. I don't fight them. This time it is easier.

It's getting late. A man in a police uniform walks into the guest house. I think he is going to arrest me and take me away from the ranch, or at least arrest Joe. For a moment, I panic at the thought of freedom. But he doesn't arrest anyone. He's here for sex, just like everyone else.

The next morning, I wake up alone. I am completely naked, and I have a massive headache. My muscles are sore, and I have bruises everywhere. There's booze in my hair and written across my abdomen in lipstick is, "Fuck-whore slave." I remember the party. The guys. The cop. *No one will ever believe me if I try to tell them. I have no one to talk to. I don't think I can do this anymore. God, I want to kill myself! Where's that bottle of Jack?*

Sixteen. The age of surrendered hope. The age of selfish sacrifice. The age of self-hatred.

"You know why we're here?" Uncle George asks me. I nod. "I have a new assignment for you, slave. This week, I want you making friends with some of these young girls out here. We're going to come home with a bigger family than what we came with." The thought of bringing anyone else into this hell makes me dizzy. I don't think I can do it. I try to remember what it feels like to be innocent. These girls look so normal. They're happy. They have friends. Families. Dreams.

"I want you to bring at least one girl back with you tonight," Uncle George says.

"How am I supposed to make friends with one of them? I don't think they will want to come with me."

"You wanna turn all the tricks yourself? Or do you want to have a break? You'll figure it out, or you'll work for two." He looks at Joe and says, "Show her how it's done."

"Come on, let's take a walk." Joe says. We walk around the campgrounds. There are horse trailers, trucks, and RVs everywhere. Young kids with ropes and cowboy boots are running around doing rope tricks. Teen girls are flirting with teen boys, and parents are busy or absent. Competitors range in age from four to forty. Dummy roping, team roping, barrel racing, calf

calf tying, even bronco and bull riding. It's a prime place for trade and a common place for meeting new people with whom to trade and travel. Families who travel the rodeo circuit live like gypsies. Common sense is a greater asset than book learning, and bringing something to the table is just as much a kid's job as an adult's. No one really cares whether or not you can read or write—many of the grown men and women in rodeo can't. That's life being raised in the saddle.

From a distance, I hear a girl screaming, "I told you, Mom. I don't want to!"

"Damn it, Anna! You're so selfish! You can stay home by yourself, then!"

"See that?" Joe asks. I look over. A girl about twelve or thirteen years old is arguing with her mother. "Wait until she storms off or her mom leaves her, then go up to her and talk to her. Tell her you know how she feels. Tell her that you don't get along with your mom, either. Then ask her if she wants to hang out with us."

I should be damned to hell for even thinking about this. I know what they are going to do with her if I bring her back. And she's going to know, too. She's going to hate me like I hate Joe. For the rest of her life, she will remember my face as the selfish bitch who sold her as a prostitute for my own freedom. I don't know if I can do it. I don't think I can, but I don't think I will make it much longer if I have to keep this up. I need a break.

I invite her to come and rodeo with us. She doesn't hesitate to follow me and trusts everything I say to her. She tells her mom she'll see her in a week, and that's the end of it. God knows if she'll ever see her again.

"Good work there, slave. I told you it wouldn't take much to bring her in. You stay in the back of the trailer with her. Tonight you'll take her pictures." Joe says. "You remember how we started you? We are going to have some fun on the Internet this evening. Tomorrow we'll start her on some real work. Let's hit the road."

I walk around back and step into the trailer. The little blonde is sitting there on the bed, looking around at the surroundings. Now I know why Joe made me make the bed and clean up the trailer this morning. "This is really nice," she says.

"Yeah. It's OK." *This feels so wrong. She has no idea.* "Your mom's not going to worry about you being with us on the road for a few weeks?"

"Nah. I leave all the time with other people. Mom's always on the road, too. If there's a rodeo I want to be part of and she doesn't want to go, I just catch a ride with somebody else. She wanted me to go with her to some place up north to sell horses, anyway. I told her I didn't want to go. She was just going to have me stay home. The neighbors are there if I need them. Anyway, she'll be happy to have some time away from me. She always wants to spend time with her new boyfriend, and I'm just in her way. I told her I wouldn't be back for a week or so. She probably won't be, either."

"Yeah, I understand. My mom has a boyfriend, too, and she doesn't exactly worry about me. It's Anna, right? How old are you?"

"Yeah. Anna. I'll be thirteen in four months."

"Cool," I say, heat radiating throughout my face. *How can I even look her in the eye? I should have never said anything to her. But if I hadn't, I'd have a quota to meet tonight—and my body still hurts from yesterday. I didn't ask for this. I shouldn't have to do it, but I don't have a choice. It's not my fault she was in the wrong place at the wrong time. God, I need to stop thinking.*

We arrive back at the ranch, and Uncle George tells Anna that she will be staying with me. He and Joe follow us to the guest house. Joe sets up the computer. "Are you ready, slave?" he asks me. Anna looks up, her face mixed with fear and confusion.

"Yeah," I say.

He hands me the camera. "Just take the basics. We'll be back for a little initiation in a few minutes."

Anna's squirming. Her eyes dart back and forth. She cracks her knuckles again and again, her foot bouncing rapidly. "Sorry, Anna, I hate to do this, but I have to take your picture. I know you probably want to run, but let's face it—there's nowhere for you to go. You don't know anyone here where we are. I'm not making you do anything I haven't already done myself. Take it from me, it's easier if you don't fight. I've earned my share of beatings, and trust me, it's not worth it." A chill runs down my back as I look down at the burn mark on my arm. I remember when I said "no." They burned me with a cattle prod lying over a bed of coals. "There's some liquor in the cabinet if you want some," I tell her.

I take the pictures of Anna. Self-hatred burns so hot that it beckons suicide. I try not to think about what I am doing. The hope of being free has been gone so long that I am blind to any chance of escape. I feel bound to what I do. The element of choice doesn't really occur to me. The pictures are like Braille—they offer me a different kind of vision. I remember Uncle George's words: "You wanna turn all the tricks yourself? Or do you want to have a break?"

I picture freedom. A night of rest. A break for my body.

Anna sits. She seems strong for a twelve-year-old. She's not crying, but her eyes are searching for understanding. "Why are you doing this? What's going to happen to me?" she asks.

"Because I don't have a choice. Someday you will understand." *What have I become?*

Joe comes back into the room. He has me go onto the computer and log into a teen chat site. The situation is all too familiar. Only this time, I am the one typing. A screen name is created: "2young4u." Immediately, private pop-up chats begin filling up the screen. Grown men from their twenties to sixties, all in a teen chat room looking for young girls. They tell us what they are looking for, and we create the scene for them. Schoolgirl. Father/daughter. Brother/sister. Teacher/student. Every imaginable forbidden sexual encounter. Most of the men have fantasies that include incest or rape. I learned quickly what they wanted, and Anna will learn, too. A dirty girl. They call us all kinds of things. Slave. Dirty whore. Bad girl. Baby. Bitch. And worse things I want so badly to forget. It's hard to feel anything but worthless when you spend your days and nights being someone's "bitch." Your only purpose is to get them off and pretend you like it.

I'm glad I'm not the one having to act out their fantasies, at least tonight. I thought I would feel better about it. I thought I would feel free. Instead, I feel even more disgusted with myself. *I'm a selfish bastard.*

Uncle George walks into the room. "Slave," he says, "Come with me." He takes me to the trailer.

"I thought I was going to get a break. You said if I brought another girl in, I would get a break."

"You did get a break. But now you have to catch up." He laughs. "You have five minutes to be ready."

Bringing Anna into the circle doesn't give me a break. We both have to work every day and every night. Looking at her is like watching what I had blocked out for so many years. Watching her smile become a scowl, her eyes become a cesspool, and her laugh—cynical mockery. I feel the fire of her hatred for me burn like a blazing backdraft. Every time we pass, I feel like the shit of the earth. But nothing compares to the acidic self-intolerance that poisons my thoughts and corrupts my entire being. In my mind, I still long for freedom. But freedom presents itself as a noose, a bottle of pills, or the cold, hard steel of a silver bullet rather than a one-way ticket home.

Summer is finally over. Uncle George drives me to the airport. Most of the trip is made in complete silence. "Two more years and we won't have to make anymore trips to the airport, eh, slave? You'll travel with us, and you can leave your past behind in Colorado. We'll take care of you here. You won't have to worry about finding some place to go, huh?"

"Yeah." I say. *Why does this feel like my only option?*

I don't want to live forever with Joe and Uncle George, but I know I'll never be able to get a place on my own. Mom has her boyfriend anyway. I can tell he doesn't really want me around. He wants me to go off somewhere to college, but I don't even think I will graduate from high school. I know what I am and what I will always be. I'm just a prostitute. Just a sex slave. A whore. No one wants me but Joe and Uncle George. Even when I'm not with them, it's like I have a stamp on my forehead that says I was made for sex. At least I know they have a place for me to live. At least I pretty much know what to expect when I'm with them. I may not be good at anything else, but at least I'm good at sex.

Uncle George parks the truck and walks me to security. "See you at Christmas time," he says to me, tipping his cowboy hat at the security officer.

I'm not sure I would have left Oregon if I had known that was the last time I would see Joe and Uncle George. Most people would guess I would scramble to get away from them, but after all those years, I felt comfortable with them. It's the fear of the unknown that scares me more than anything. Life isn't good by any definition of the word, but it is predictable. Things could be worse somewhere else. Joe always tells me it's better to work for him and Uncle George than it is to work for somebody who isn't family. He reminds me how well they take care of me and that others might not treat me as well. It isn't that I like what I do—in fact, I hate it. Every day I live with the notion that I am just a worthless whore, and if ever I forget that, Joe is sure to remind me of my place and purpose in the world. But at least I *have* a purpose—even if it isn't the best kind, it's better than nothing at all. I know I can wake up each day and expect the same thing. I don't have to guess what is going to happen to me; I know. That makes me feel like I have some kind of control over my life. At the end of the night, no matter who I have been with, I know where I am going to end up—in the trailer or on the ranch, and that is the closest thing to peace I can find. After all I've been through, Uncle George and Joe have never left me. I can trust them.

When I return to Colorado, I can't stop thinking about Anna. *She was a normal kid, and I messed her up. She could have grown up to have a normal life—a job and a family, but now she'll never know that.* Uncle George convinces Anna's mom she will be successful with him. He can take her to rodeos and allow her to participate in competitions while Aunt Lisa home-schools Anna and Joe. I traded Anna in for my own freedom, and the worst part is, I'm still not free. I never got my end of the deal.

I start doing coke to help me cope. It makes it easier for me to forget what I don't want to remember. It keeps me up all night, then during the day, I just sleep. If I go to class, I sleep through it. One of my teachers expresses some concerns she has, after a world geography class.

"Kate, are you doing OK?" she asks. She stares, waiting for a response. "Kate!"

I stare down at my hands, picking at the hangnails on my fingers.

"Kate, I am talking to you!"

I don't hear anyone call me. I am busy in thought, dissociated from the present. Finally, the teacher shakes my shoulder with her hand. "Kate, are you doing all right?"

"Yeah, I'm fine." *Kate. Nobody has called me that in a long time.* Mom never calls me anything but "honey" or "baby," and she calls everybody that. *Kate.* I laugh aloud.

"Is something funny?" She asks. *Hardly. She has no idea who I am.*

"Is there something you want from me?"

"You're looking awfully gaunt," she says. "And it's a little warm for you to still be wearing sweats and a sweatshirt."

"I get cold easily," I say. *Gaunt? Good. Maybe I will slowly disappear and everyone will just leave me alone. What does she care about me, anyway?*

"I've seen you sitting during the lunch hour. Do you ever eat lunch?"

"Yeah, I eat lunch." I lie. *Nobody wants to be with a scrawny woman.* I try to keep emotions from my face, but I'm relieved to know that I am getting smaller.

"OK," she says.

I head out the door toward the stairwell to make my way to the next class. Suddenly, my eyes go blurry, and my head starts to spin. I wake up in the nurse's office.

"Where's my sweatshirt?!" I ask in a panic.

"We have it over here," the nurse says. "Why don't you sit up? Here, eat this granola bar. You are looking very pale."

"Um, no thanks. I'm not hungry."

"I didn't ask if you were hungry. Eat it. You passed out; it could very likely be from low blood sugar."

"I don't want it." Her eyes narrow as she looks at me.

"How about you step over here so I can get your height and weight?"

"Do I really have to do that?"

"Yes. I would like to write your information in your report here." I slip off of the cot and stand against the wall.

"Five-two," she says. "Now, step on the scale, please." I step on the scale. "Seventy-nine pounds. That's hardly substantial for a high-school student, don't you think, Kate?" I shrug. She picks up the phone and dials a number.

"Hello, is this Kate's mother? Yes, I am going to need you to come to the school and pick her up. She passed out not too long ago, and we need you to take her in for a physical and psychological checkup before she returns to school. We'll need the results before she returns to classes."

I don't go back to my classes, and I don't go back to Oregon that Christmas either. After my physical and psychological examination, some information is reported to Child Protective Services. I tell them of many things, but I do not tell them about what happened to me in Oregon. When they confront my mother about my physical and emotional well-being, she is furious. Mostly out of self-preservation, I think. She seems angry at me for refusing to eat. I don't think she understands it isn't that simple. I know she cares about me and wants me to be healthy, but I think she is relieved when she is asked to find a place for me to go where I can receive inpatient care. She doesn't know how to take care of me, and she doesn't understand why I have issues. Probably because she does, too. She just can't admit it.

I leave home and am enrolled in an inpatient care facility. Things are different from the beginning. They label everything. The bins beneath my bed have my name on them. My prescriptions, my student handbook, my locker space—everything says "Kate." Everyone calls me "Kate." It's weird at first. I have to think to respond, but it feels so good to hear my name.

They don't know what I am here. They don't know who I am. I can be Kate and they would never know the difference. I smile. *It will be easy living here.*

But rehab isn't easy. No one knows anything about me. That feels so good that I am afraid to spoil it. I worry about what they will think if they knew the real me. *Would it spoil my "fresh start?"* I want someone to love me *after* they know who I am and what I have done, not when they don't know me at all. But I am too afraid to lose the love I am experiencing for the first time.

I start counseling and am able to open up about some of the things I experienced, but I dumb it down and make it much simpler than it really was. They know I have been abused. They know I have experimented with drugs and alcohol. They know I have an eating disorder. They know Kate, but they don't know that calling me by that name is a resurrection of my innocence and, on their part, complete ignorance of the last eight years of my life. They don't know I am a sex slave. They don't know that Kate hasn't existed for the last eight years.

The longer I am there, the more I test the waters. I tell them a piece of my past and gauge their response to see if they can handle it, or if they believe me. I begin the process of treatment.

The recovery process is long, and although I am out of rehab, I am still recovering. But I am safe from Joe. I am safe from Uncle George. I wish, though, that I were safe from everyone else. From their assumptions. From their questions. From their judgment.

I live in a world where I have to hide who I am and what I have gone through. In certain settings, I have made myself vulnerable to share small bits of my story. I'm not in physical danger anymore, but the pain is often still unbearable. Certain simple things flood back the memories. Words and phrases such as "little girl," "you get what you pay for," "daddy," "shhh...everyone is sleeping," or the mention of particular places. Certain scents—manure, tobacco, and particular colognes. Certain sights—a cowboy hat, a police officer, coiled ropes, horses, chewing tobacco at the register of a gas station, the exchange of money. These things quench my spirit and pain my soul. When I am asked if I am OK, there is no appropriate response but to lie.

I cannot share my past with most people. They just wouldn't understand. And even on the rare occasion I open up in the slightest, the response I receive is a load of questions. Simple questions. Common questions. Painful questions. "Why didn't you tell someone?" "Why didn't you call the police?" "Why did you go back?" "Why didn't you turn them in?" Valid questions, I guess, to a person who doesn't understand, but wounding questions to a victim of violence. These questions insinuate that I could have ended the abuse at any point in time, that I chose it for myself, that I never tried to escape—or worse, that it was either consensual or a lie (otherwise I would have reported it). These are the questions that simplify what is not simple at all. These are the questions of an individual who has never been beaten, broken, and brutalized; silenced, drugged, or locked up; burned, cut, or on the hollow end of a gun barrel. These are the questions of one who has never seen an officer, politician, or respected husband and father in the back room of a brothel.

It has been eight years. I am a good mother, a loving wife, and a hard worker. I have educated myself—read many books, studied many things, and even attended college. I have a good home and a good life, far from where my worst memories took place. Even so, I have no decent stories to tell my daughter about my childhood.

Uncle George went to prison for several years on separate charges but was never prosecuted for human trafficking. He has since been released from prison. I can only assume he is continuing to run underage prostitution rings. Law enforcement was informed about Joe's involvement, but he never was charged and was excused as a minor—he never even went to trial. There have since been accusations made against him, but no convictions.

I will never be able to forget what happened throughout my childhood and adolescent years, but by God's grace, I have been given a new life, and I won't throw it away. Every day I become less of a slave, and I find out more about who Kate really is. No one knows my whole story. No one but me and God Himself.

Some people say that God's love is unconditional. It's a good thing, too, because any love with conditions would never make it past the first chapter of my life. But God has said in His Word, "I have loved you…with an everlasting love. With unfailing love I have drawn you to myself" (Jeremiah 31:3). And *that* is enough for me to keep on going. *Someone* knows me— *all of me*—and still loves me completely.

KATE'S VOICE

Words To the Wise

As much as you possibly can, try not to place victims or perpetrators into stereotypical boxes. It is important to know what to look for when trying to identify victims of sexual exploitation and perpetrators; look for signs (victim not having any identification, never being left alone, bruises, signature tattoo markings or brandings, avoidance of open communication, person being unaware of her exact location, etc.) rather than stereotypical profiles. Almost every instance of human trafficking will have at least one big element that doesn't fit the "profile." A few details from my own story that don't fit the profile are that one of my traffickers was younger than I was. Also, I was trafficked in rural areas more often than I was in the city. Forms of payment were many times on the service/barter system rather than purely monetary. I was trafficked through a family member and not kidnapped off the street. My trafficker did not look or dress any different than people surrounding him. Those who purchase sex are no different than some of the people you connect with every day—they are husbands, businesspeople, men, women, young, old, and lower, middle, and upper class. Human trafficking is no respecter of persons.

Many times when people imagine a victim of human trafficking, they imagine a young, pretty, innocent-looking girl who is frail and crying out to be rescued. In the beginning, that's how I looked, but that quickly changed. It is important to remember that victims of human trafficking have been forced to age beyond their years due to constant physical and sexual abuse, they likely will not trust the first (or tenth) person who wants to "help" them or "rescue" them, and they may appear to be more comfortable or content in the role that was assigned to them than you would imagine. If you can recognize a "prostitute" but not a human-trafficking victim, I challenge you to let go of "natural" perceptions and recognize that they often are inaccurate. We cannot identify true colors through tinted glasses. It is very uncommon that a woman, young or old, actually chose to become a prostitute. Most prostitutes were victims of sexual violence. We must challenge ourselves to treat every person and case uniquely, and be willing to learn the entirety of every case/story.

Prevention

I believe the key to prevention is awareness and involvement. Every person is responsible for his or her own role, whether as a parent, guardian, mentor, or career person. We all have a responsibility to educate ourselves within our field. Parents are responsible for protecting their children, as are teachers, social workers, counselors, youth leaders, medical professionals, and law enforcement officers. Medical professionals can be trained to identify marks and signs of physical and sexual abuse. If teachers are involved in their students' lives, they can notice changes in behavior, grades, or temperament. Social workers, youth workers, and counselors can learn the right questions to ask children if they see or hear of any cause for concern to make sure that their clients/kids are in a safe, nonabusive environment. Often, children/ teenagers who are acting out for attention or exhibiting delinquent behaviors are doing so because of unseen/unknown problems and abuse in the home. It is important to note that most trafficking victims have experienced prior physical/sexual/psychological abuse, and a high number are or were in foster care and are runaways. A key to prevention is working with these children/teens to find a safe environment for them, as well as counseling/ coaching *before* they become victims of human trafficking.

In my situation and in many others, professionals were either unaware or aware and uninvolved. Lack of awareness and lack of involvement are equally detrimental in assisting a child who is being trafficked or at risk of being trafficked. Attend a seminar or conference on human trafficking, look into your state's policies and laws regarding human trafficking, and encourage policy changes that address the issue. Request a training event for community members or professionals in your sphere of influence.

Maintaining Freedom

Maintaining freedom and finding wholeness has not been easy. I have been out of "the life" for years, actively seeking healing through counseling, groups, and programs, and I am still far from the end. Some days I have wanted to give up—after eight years of constant attempts to find wholeness, I am tired. Tired of fighting the flashbacks. Tired of going to counseling. Tired of warding off painful memories, fears, and anger every time I try to be intimate. There are days when I have wondered if it is really possible to ever be free from the person I was forced to be. I am still learning to trust and to live life like a "normal person." Most days, it takes more effort than I care to admit. Sometimes people have said, "Wow, I would have never been able to guess that you had gone through anything like this. You seem so normal." In those moments, I feel both relieved and anguished; accepted and alone. If only they had a glimpse of the battle that rages inside me every single day. I long for the day when the person who I appear to be on the outside is wholly and completely who I am on the inside. People who ask, "How did you get out?" don't get it. "Getting out" is a lifelong process. Recovery is a lifelong process. I used to beat myself up for still struggling. Now I realize that trauma impacts people. As I grow and heal, I don't have to allow trauma to control or influence me as much, but it never completely goes away. There will always be triggers and painful memories, but I am learning to respond to my triggers and memories differently.

Another hurdle was learning to take care of myself. Because my experiences took place when I was so young, I lacked a lot of life skills that most people learn growing up. I didn't know how to cook, clean, drive, or balance a checkbook. I had extreme anxiety about talking on the phone or face-to-face with people, and that made it difficult for me to schedule appointments or do a job interview. A huge step toward maintaining my freedom is becoming independent. Simple things, such as learning how to drive, learning a new job, graduating from high school (I had dropped out), and continuing my education, were very empowering for me in my recovery.

Having a mentor who knew my weaknesses and was not afraid to love me through them and call me out on them was also important. Knowing I can always contact her when I am having a moment of irrational thinking or need advice and encouragement has helped tremendously. I have also found that the more I share my story, the less power it has over me.

Allowing my past to have purpose (sharing it to educate or inspire others who have experienced hardship) has helped me transform from a victim to an overcomer. I am not a victim anymore. I *was* a victim. Now, I choose to let my life have purpose, and I make my own decisions. When I am helping other people, I find that the worthless feeling I used to have dissipates, and I am not as tempted to return to a mediocre life. When I gave birth to my daughter, my world was completely changed. I know I can't go back to my old life—she needs me, and I want her to grow up with dignity. I will work hard to be an example for her.

Within forty-eight hours of running away one in three adolescents will likely be solicited for commercial sex.

Chapter 5

SURVIVAL SEX AND MALE EXPLOITATION

THE STORY YOU ARE about to read has two major themes: survival sex due to homelessness and the seldom-documented, commercial sexual exploitation of a male. We will take a look at both.

The Issue of Homelessness

"I'm amazed when I look back at the things I could do when I was high…" After several years, I became numb to the idea of sexual bartering. Turning a trick was the same as going and eating a hamburger."

—Homeless youth, living on the streets since age ten[1]

Within forty-eight hours of running away, one in three adolescents likely will be solicited for commercial sexual exploitation, with an estimated 60 percent of runaway or throwaway youth at risk overall.[2] "Throwaways" are defined as kids forced to leave home or prevented from returning home. In this overview, I use the term "runaway" to refer to both runaway and throwaway youth.[3] A large number of runaways suffer from abuse and neglect in the home and are not typically running "to the streets" but rather "from home."

Once on the street, these youth are left to fend for themselves, with an estimated 70 percent engaging in "survival sex," defined as the exchange of sex to meet basic needs such as food, shelter, clothing, drugs, or money.[4] Many homeless youth come from chaotic and dysfunctional families. Due to this lack of parental guidance, homeless youth often lack the problem-solving and conflict-resolution skills needed to survive on the streets. This makes them highly susceptible to the dangers associated with survival sex: STDs, rape, and murder.

Squat houses are commonly used by homeless youth. Featurepics.com.

"I remember my first experience working with street kids. It was twenty years ago, and I was a young and undertrained volunteer helping at a youth shelter in Washington state. The kids came to the drop-in shelter periodically to get a hot meal or a good night's sleep. The rules were few: Follow the curfew and no weapons. In keeping with the rules, the kids would leave their guns and knives in the bushes outside until they left. Once I became a familiar face, the kids began to trust me with their stories. The stories were similar; these kids were staying in abandoned buildings called "squats," controlled by men or women expecting some sort of sexual payment in return. The majority of these kids were engaged in survival sex—trading sex, the only thing they had to offer, for food and a place to sleep for the night. Sadly, twenty years ago, no one was talking about the commercial exploitation of children or survival sex among homeless populations, and we were ill-equipped to help them. If only we knew then what we know now!"

—Alisa Jordheim, founder, Justice Society

Creating Family

Just like the kids I worked with in Washington, most runaway youth congregate in urban areas.[5] They tend to migrate in groups and move along a circuit from city to city, staying until pressure from local law enforcement gets too "hot." One study shows that 54 percent of homeless youth form close social networks of several individuals they call "brothers." With limited biological connections, street kids form their own variation of family relationships. One young man shares the sense of family he felt on the street:

> *"When you go through some of the things that we went through, it's like going through a war together or something. You start to feel intensely about everyone in the group. You'd just do anything for them.... We would always be looking out for each other."* [6]

Despite the distinction in the law, the line between survival sex and sex trafficking is somewhat fluid because survival sex often leads to trafficking victimization. Ruby's story, which follows, demonstrates how her initial experiences of survival sex led directly to human trafficking:

> *Starting at age five, Ruby was repeatedly raped by her brother's father. By eighteen, she was on her own and low on money. About once a month, when she needed money to pay the rent, she would negotiate with men to exchange sex for money. At nineteen, she was heading out to a party with what she thought was a group of new friends when she found herself alone in her room with one of them. The man pulled a gun on her and stated that he was a pimp and that from now on she should call him 'daddy.' "I remember thinking, Is this real? Pimps are for real? I didn't think pimps existed anywhere but the movies before then." For the following three months, Ruby was forced to sleep with "too many men to count" and was watched every second. At some*

point, she gained the trust of the woman in charge of guarding her, and Ruby was able to make her escape.[7]

MALE EXPLOITATION

How real is the problem of commercial sexual exploitation of boys in America? Information suggests that 10 to 50 percent of exploited youth are male.[8] It is hard to get a clear picture of the extent of the issue because most boys do not self-identify as victims. This lack of self-identification is often fueled by the shame and stigma associated with male sexual exploitation—labeling the child as gay.

Gender Affiliation

There is a common misconception that the most sexually exploited boys are homosexual, bisexual, or transgender. Studies show that the majority of victimized boys are heterosexual, with only 25 to 35 percent self-identifying as gay, bisexual, or transgender.[9] There are several other key distinctions between the trafficking experiences of boys and girls. As referenced in Chapter 1, research indicates that boys and transgender youth in the United States are trafficked at slightly younger ages than girls—boys and transgender youth between the ages of eleven and thirteen; girls between twelve and fourteen.[10] Boys are also considered to have a disproportionately higher rate of illicit drug use.[11]

On October 31, 2013, Marc Branch was indicted by a New Jersey grand jury on charges of human trafficking, engaging in prostitution with a person younger than eighteen, and other offenses related to exploitation of young men. As in Mr. Branch's story, it is thought that approximately 95 percent of sexual exploiters of boys are adult males, many married with children.[12]

"It is alleged that Branch lured vulnerable young men, ranging in age from their teens to their early twenties, to his apartment by offering them money, drugs, friendship, and, in some instances, shelter. He allegedly targeted victims who were estranged from their families. He allegedly gave the young victims drugs and alcohol, fueling their drug dependency, so that he could control them and prostitute them to male clients, who paid up to $200 to engage in a sexual act."[13]

No Pimps Allowed

Only a small percentage of male youth are trafficked by a pimp. Boys tend to work independently and are typically propositioned on the street directly by a buyer or through online and magazine ads.[14] Sexually exploited boys call themselves "hustlers." This term implies that they are "putting one over" on the johns and in control of the sexual transactions.[15] Those few who do work under the control of a trafficker are extremely difficult to identify by law enforcement. Traffickers are known to require a "buyer" to perform a sexual act with the child in the presence of the trafficker. Because law enforcement officers cannot comply with this requirement, the trafficker can quickly identify a "true customer" from an undercover agent. Traffickers are said to take these extra precautions when trafficking boys because men arrested for trafficking young boys are labeled "short eyes" in the jail systems and suffer extreme hostility from other inmates.[16]

The secrecy and lack of support services associated with the commercial sexual exploitation of boys make it difficult to track and document. People do not typically think of boys as victims of this crime; therefore, the signs of abuse frequently go unnoticed.[17] Sadly, boys are often considered as an afterthought in the fight against commercial sexual exploitation of children. One article said it well: A panel discussion about commercial sexual exploitation often ends with the words "...and boys, too." [18]

There Is Hope

"I'd been on the streets for over two years, and the shame and disap-pointment made it difficult to even look at myself in the mirror. But that's all changed. Over the past year, I've been on the road to recovery, and I now volunteer at a local drop-in center. The guys I used to hang with on the street now ask me, "How did you do it? Do you think I can get out, too?' I say, 'Man, if I can do it, anyone can—you can, too!' I'm a changed man, and I love the person I am now."

—Mike Gould, survivor

The Inside Story

It took more than two years to find a man willing and able to meet the criteria for participating in this book project. The requirements were rigorous, and in Rich's case, we had to make some exceptions. Rich was actually eigh-teen years old when he was first trafficked in Montreal, Canada, and then returned home to Providence, Rhode Island. His story is an accurate depic-tion of what life on the streets is like and is very similar to that of many commercially sexually exploited, homeless children.

I want to express my gratitude to Rich for his courageous commitment to share his story, giving us a rare glimpse into what young men face while being exploited on the streets.

Rich is a cofounder of Project Weber, a nonprofit organization committed to improving the health and well-being of male sex workers in Providence, Rhode Island.

PROVIDENCE
By Luke Robert Miller

"Rich, honey, snack's ready," Mom announces as she rolls her wheelchair to the sink. While she cleans the sticky bowl, I look at her long, brown hair and think about how pretty she is—even if she is handicapped. I survey the room: the old, worn, wooden cabinets; the bare brass handles; and that floor that is perfect for wearing socks on! Sliiddee!

Before sitting down, I shove three cookies into my mouth. Being a little kid has its perks.

"Honey, Grandma will be here soon to visit," my mother says gently while drying the now-clean bowl. "I know you're excited, Rich, but slow down before you choke."

I smile, displaying a mouth filled with chocolate chunks. My mother is one of two people in my life who I know truly loves me. The other person is on her way to my house: *Grandma*!

The doorbell rings.

I just grin as I stand between Mom and the door she is now trying to open.

"Hello, honey," Grandma says to my mom.

"Hello, Mother."

"Grandma!" I scream.

"Well, who do we have here?" she coyly responds.

"It's Rich!" I say, pointing to myself with two hands.

"Rich, you say? I am not sure I know anyone named Rich." Her speech slows as if she is scrolling through her ancient memory.

Still pointing at myself, I franticly announce, "It's me, Grandma! It's your Cutie Pie!"

"Oh! Yes, yes, I believe I do recall that name. I am pretty sure it is on this big red package that I found outside on your porch." She winks at me as she leans down and kisses my forehead. "I love you, Rich! This is for you!"

"I love you, too, Grandma!" I say as I hug her leg.

When the furious tornado of wrapping paper, tape, and cardboard subsides, there is a little five-year-old boy sitting on the floor with a brilliant red truck.

"Where are you, Rich? " Grandma asks.

I peek out from under the mess of wrapping paper and cardboard, pushing around my new, shiny, red truck.

"Vroom, vroooom! Here I am, Grandma."

Grandma laughs, looks at Mom, and says, "He still has the fasteners around the wheels."

They both laugh.

Where Is Love To Be Found?

My mom is a good person. I love her very much. But I have to wonder, why did she ever marry my dad?

"Mom," I mumble during bath time.

"Yes?"

"Vrooommmm." My truck is making an amphibious assault on the Floating Duck Army. "Do you love Dad?"

"Of course," she says. "That's not a question for a six-year-old little boy, Rich."

"OK." Duck one is plunged to his death from the Tub Edge Cliffs. "Sometimes I wonder if he loves me."

"Sometimes I wonder if he loves me, too," falls off her lips faintly. "Rich," Mom says as she wheels her chair closer to the tub, "you need to wash your hair."

"Mom?" I say.

"Yes, honey, what is it now?"

"Ummm, did Daddy put you in that chair?"

"No, honey. Your dad has never hurt me. I had a tumor. Do you know what that is?"

I shake my head no, and small suds float off of my hair.

"Well, a tumor is like a big bump or a ball that grows in your body."

"Is it bad?"

"Yes, honey, very bad. During the operation to take the tumor out, my back was hurt, and I never walk... "

I lie back, thrusting my hair under the water. The sound rushes over my ears. I can see Mom sitting over me. Why does Mom have to be broken? Why does Dad have to hurt me? In my mind, my father's words swirl in my head: "Faggot." "Lazy." "Piece of shit." Maybe I am broken, too?

I grab my truck, sit up, and jump out of the water. "'Til we meet again, Floating Duck Army!"

Like Father, Like Son?

Dad cracks open another beer. He slurps foam off the top, announcing, "Go play with your dolls, ya little faggot."

"Where's Mom?" I sheepishly ask my father.

"Where do you think?" he barks at me. "The hospital!"

I stand in silence, gripping my truck. *What should I do?* I think. *She can't leave me here with him. But she leaves me here every time she goes to the hospital.*

"Oh," I say and look down.

"If I'm lucky, she'll die! I'll be free of the shackle!"

"What's a shackle?" I ask as a tear rolls down my face.

"Are you cryin'?" "You lil' faggot! You and your mommy! Geett over here," he slurs.

He's been drinking. I want to run. I freeze dead in my tracks. I look down.

"Look at me when I am talking to you! Dammit, kid, look at me!" he screams, removing his belt slowly and methodically, looking dead into my eyes.

"Y-y-y-yes, sir," I stammer as I slowly tilt my head upward from his belt to catch his violent gaze. Just as I tilt my head up, I catch something from the corner of my eye. I hear the sound as if it comes from somewhere distant, not yet comprehending what's happened. Startled, I try to pick myself up; my face is on fire. *Was that a belt?* I think. I tilt my head up again just in time to be cracked across the head a second time. Yes, that is a belt. I stagger backward to create distance between the two of us. He lunges for me. I throw myself behind the recliner and cover my head. I plead, "I'm sorry, Daddy, I'm sorry. I won't do it again! It was my fault. Please, please!" Tears streak down my face. I begin to count in my mind, "One, two, three, four ..."

I wake up. *Where am I?* Looking up, I see him victoriously bring the beer to his lips. He takes a deep breath. "Glad to see you're awake again. Your aunt and uncle will be here at four. Be ready and packed. You're staying with them 'til your mother is out of the hospital. I can't have you here. Your mother spoiled you. You're weak, and I don't have time to take care of another invalid." He spits wildly, and it hits me right in the face.

While packing, I think, *Any place must be better than this one. I just wish my mom was here. I wish my mom wasn't paralyzed.* I bow my head so that my father won't see me crying.

Family Ties

Where am I? I think. I rub my eyes. Immediately, fear grips me, and I reach my hands under the covers. *There it is.* Relief settles as I pull my toy from the bed. I speak to the person in the bed next to me. "Auntie?"

"Huh?"

"I'm hungry."

"Go make yourself something." She rolls away from me.

"But Auntie, I am too little to cook!"

"Shit, kid. Auntie's head hurts. Go watch TV or something."

I pull my truck close, trying to ignore the naked body pressed against mine. At least it's finally daytime. Daytime is much safer than nighttime.

I pull myself from the bed and make my way, hungry and tired, to the television. After two episodes of *Scooby-Doo* and one episode of *The Smurfs*, Auntie finally appears.

"Turn that down." She pulls a bottle from the freezer and pours the clear liquid into a glass of orange juice.

"Make me one," I hear from behind. "Hi, sport," he says to me with a wink. My stomach hurts.

Forcing a smile, I nod. In my head, I keep thinking, *Why is he naked? I hate it here.* There aren't any beatings, but this is just as uncomfortable.

"Here's your eggs." I take the plate from my Auntie, who now has her robe belt undone.

I survey my surroundings while silently eating. This apartment is much smaller than my parents' house. But I like the plush carpet. It's an old, dirty green. It feels good on my feet as I sit chewing my eggs. I look at the pictures of my aunt and uncle as kids. From the corner of my eye, I see that my aunt's robe is open. *Yuck.*

Why do they do that in front of me? It makes my tummy hurt. I glance over across the breakfast bar again and catch a glimpse of them kissing each other. This is gross. Why is he licking her? I'm never going to kiss anyone like that. I need to get away from this. I am looking for an escape when I hear, "Why do you look so sad, honey? You don't like watching the love your auntie and uncle have?" Her hands are violating my uncle right in front of me.

"I don't feel well." Thinking quickly, I add, "I think I need to use the bathroom." That should definitely get me out of here for a while. I begin moving toward the bathroom.

"Honey," Auntie says.

"Yes?" I answer.

"When you are done, come into the bedroom."

I slump.

What can I do? Holding my breath, I begin counting: One, two, three, four...

I Am Ten

"Mom?"

"Yes, honey?"

"I need to tell you something." I look at her wheelchair. "We watched a film in school this morning about molestation."

She stops. I have her attention now.

"Ummm...." I trail off. "The things they said in this movie—they've happened to me."

"What?" she responds, confused.

"Auntie," I whisper.

"Oh, I see."

"She kissed me on the mouth, and she and Uncle touched me." I can't help but look down. I am sweating. "Like on TV."

"Well, you know how Auntie is when she drinks," Mother says dismissively.

"But they're always walking around naked. And they touch me...."

"Rich, they've been so good to take care of you when I'm in the hospital. I think you're just overreacting," she responds.

What happened to my mother's attention? Why can't she just save me for once? I run as fast as I can through the door and down the block.

The Running Continues

I have been running for years, I think as we escape.

"Dude, that was sick!"

"I told you these faggots have nothing on us!" As the words leave my mouth, my father's words ring in my head, *"Ya little faggot."*

"Hell, yes!" I smile widely to cover the voice in my head.

"You two run fast," we hear from behind as Jim bends over, heaving. "I can't believe you meet all these faggots at the train station. Is it like a Gay Train Station?" In an announcer's voice, he says, "Come ride us. We promise you'll enjoy it!"

I half laugh at this humor to conceal my own identity. "That faggot we just kicked the shit out of," I point behind Jim and Brad, "I've seen that pervert taking a fifteen-year-old boy home from the station. Sick pedo! He won't be molesting any more kids for a while."

We all laugh.

It's just a typical day in class, and I'm handing in another pointless assignment. My paper's titled "What happens when the people you are 'running to' are actually those you are 'running from'?" Just reading the title seems to make my teacher, Mr. Craig, seethe.

"I should have known that you wouldn't be able to do the assignment correctly." He stands up, looks me in the eyes, and walks to the trash can.

I won't give this jerk the vindication of letting him know that I spent the evening getting my ass whipped by a drunk who marauds as my "father." I won't tell Mr. Craig that his assignment is a waste. I won't tell him that all I can think of is running away—escaping the beatings. "Go play with your dolls..."—my father's voice echoes in my head.

In midthought, I hear Principal Higgins call Mr. Craig to the hallway. As I elbow Jim, I say, "Watch this!"

With my hands in my pockets and everyone's eyes locked on me, I stand up. I whistle lightly and turn slowly, checking the front, the back, the sides. All clear. Giggling to myself, I draw a perfect elephant's trunk with two large coconuts under it. My classmates' cackles fill my ears. I begin a near-perfect caricature of Mr. Craig, including his giant forehead, elongated, my artistic license at work. Proud, I stand back and admire how my art classes have paid off.

"Rich!" I hear from somewhere behind me.

I whirl around to see both Mr. Craig and Mr. Higgins staring at me. Mr. Craig's face is red with rage.

"That's it, Rich. Come with me."

The class bursts into laughter as I follow Principal Higgins out the door. I take a short bow, wink at Mary, and blow a kiss to Mr. Craig.

The Refuge of Friendship

"How did you learn how to draw like that?" Jim asks, smiling at me approvingly.

"Where does this guy live?" comes Brad's voice, obviously not listening.

"Two blocks this way," Jim chimes in, pointing his finger.

"Art class," I state frankly.

"You go to art class?" They both look surprised.

"For the last two years I have." I have their attention. "It's pretty awesome. Last week we got to make our own prints. I took the LA Gear logo from my shoe and made it into a T-shirt."

"Nice."

"Shit, man! That is rad!"

They are obviously impressed. I'm like a chameleon. I make sure to fit into any group. This way no one will know who I really am. I know I don't.

"I think this is it," Brad says, handing me back the piece of paper on which I had written the address.

Our attention turns to the house in front of us. It is a white, comely home with dirty, green shutters. "His name is Javier," I announce to no one and everyone.

"You said he would have beer," Jim asserts.

"I don't know, man. I met this guy at the East Side train station where I grab the bus to get to art class. He always just chills there."

"He a faggot?" Jim obviously remembers the pedo from last week.

"Nah, Jim. I mean, I don't think he is." I try to maintain the authority of group leader as I wonder what I may be getting us into.

Once inside, the party is going. "Here you go," Javier says as he hands a beer to Brad. "Rich, glad you could make it!" He holds out two beers in the same hand. Jim and I each grab one. "To getting whacked!"

This room is old and musty, I think through my fourteen-year-old brain, which is affected by my fifth beer. The only way to describe these furnishings is "sixties." This is definitely better from the outside than the inside. The twenty or so people here all seem to be young. Only two are girls.

All of a sudden, Javier grabs my hand and pulls me toward the living room. I yank my hand away quickly as I follow him around the couch, doing my best to balance. I wonder, *How long have I been here?*

"I have something that will change your life." He smiles at me as I take the seat beside him on the couch.

"OK," I say suspiciously.

He hands me a thin tube with a round cutout in the end, similar to any pipe you'd use to smoke weed. He drops a small, yellowish rock into the pipe.

"What is it?" I hear myself ask through the fog of alcohol.

I hear nothing in response. I take my first hit.

"What time is it?"

"It's two," comes the response from a vaguely familiar voice.

I look up and ask, "A.M.?"

Javier smiles down at me. "No, P.M."

"What?" I am so lost right now. "Is it Sunday? Have I been here all night?"

He laughs loudly. I can hardly contain how annoyed I am right now.

"No, it's Tuesday. I told you it would change your life. I never lie!"

I refuse to speak to this jerk. After surveying the room for my friends and finding that they aren't here, I gather myself. "Javier, what the hell was that?"

"Crack."

The words echo in my head. Did I really just take crack?

Finding My Place

For the entirety of my sixteen years of life, I have been seeking a way to erase my past so that I may become all that I know I am. I am seeking to right the wrongs that have been perpetrated against me. My mind swirls amid the thoughts of the past: *"Ya little faggot." "Why is he naked?" "She's a victim, too."*

As I reach in my pocket, I look for the thing I need most. Where is it? "There you are!" I pull a hard rock from my pocket. Some people don't believe in love at first sight, but I have been in love with crack since our first meeting at Javier's house. I inhale as deeply as I can. Within seconds, it becomes apparent that nothing can stop me. I am invincible!

I look at everyone on the floor of this trap house[*], lifeless bodies strewn about. Two kids, little girls, in a corner play with a makeshift doll. I smile. I reach in my pocket and pull out a half-eaten pack of crackers. "Do you need some food?"

The girl with the brown hair nods yes. The blond-haired girl seems to avoid my gaze at all costs. I hand the three orange crackers with peanut butter in the middle to the brown-haired girl. She slowly reaches forward, takes the crackers, and hides them under her shirt. *It really feels good to help*, I think. I grab my bag and head out to "the rest of my life."

In thirty minutes, my new job at Subway starts! This is my fourth job in three months. I don't need much to survive. I can always find a couch to crash on or a squat house to catch some shut-eye in. If worse comes to worst, I can go home and sleep there for a few nights. But things haven't been safe since I quit school.

With my seventeenth birthday approaching next month, I want to save up money and get out of Dodge!

---

[*] Trap house: A crack house or the surroundings that a drug dealer, or "trap star," would use to make his or her profit.

"Hey," I say as I enter Subway. I have been working here for six months, and I have managed to save almost four hundred bucks, spending the remainder on crack. I have noticed that I am spending more and more on drugs these days. But I have it under control. It is just nice to avoid life once in a while. I think I will stop doing drugs when I go to New York City.

My Descent

I'm ready for a fresh start. For five months, I haven't touched crack, I've got my shit together, I found an apartment, and I even started a new gig at a home improvement store. But life here in Providence has become a little mundane.

As an escape, I've been planning this trip to New York City for months. Last summer, I was there for a concert; the people and the culture spoke to me. Finally on my way, I lean back in my seat on the bus to get comfy for the long ride. After checking into a hotel, I focus my endeavors on exploring this amazing city! I walk down the street, feeling immediately dizzy in the shadow of the high-rises. *I love this city.*

Buzzzzzzzzz goes the alarm. *It's too early. Where is the aspirin?* I'm greeted by a headache that serves as evidence of last night's overindulgence.

Shower. Shave. Pack, one item at a time, folded, placed neatly in my bag. *It's been a great week, but I have to leave today*, I sadly inform myself.

I wedge my foot in the door to gain leverage, hoisting my bag around the bed and out the door. Once I'm outside the hotel, I spot a young man, no older than seventeen, approaching me. He looks disheveled and lost. "Hello," I say as a courtesy.

"Hey, man. Is there any way you could spare me some change? I am hungry. Please, man, I would really appreciate it."

"No, you're not."

"What? Seriously, I am hungry. I haven't eaten in days. I am away from home, and I need to buy a ticket home...."

"You don't have to lie. What are you on?"

"What?"

"I'm not a cop or a narc. I am not even from New York." I take a moment so he can comprehend what I am saying. "If you are honest, I promise to make it worth your while."

"Crack," he states more directly than I'm prepared for. My mind immediately goes back to Javier's, the trap house, my father, my aunt, my mother. *"Ya lil' faggot."* Maybe he isn't lying. I smirk. I continue walking as he paces beside me. Clearly, he notices that I am mulling this over. I see myself in this boy. "How about this?" I inquire. "You find someone who will sell us weed, and I will pay for the weed. We can share it!" He smiles back at me when I tell him this. "I will even buy you dinner, too, once our appetites kick in. What do you think? Deal?"

He leers at me suspiciously. I can see trust isn't something this kid has in abundance. In the end, like a true addict, he says, "Yes, I'm in."

We walk down the street. "I'm Rich," I state without looking at him.

"David," he says without glancing in my direction, either. "You stay here?" he asks more curtly than I think he intends. The paranoia that goes hand in hand with crack is not foreign to me.

"This is the place," he says. I hand him a twenty. "Wait here." He disappears into the house.

Just get the pot and get out of here, I think as I sit down on the curb.

"He didn't have any," David says, walking up to me. He places a dime bag of crack in my hand.

Did he really get turned down for weed? I contemplate. Whatever his reason, David has me. I salivate just holding it.

Behind the hotel, I take the pipe from David. I swallow. "OK," I quietly mutter. "Let's do this."

A smile immediately spreads across David's grim face. He pats my shoulder approvingly. I nod solemnly. The alley behind the hotel is dimly lit. I am conscious enough to notice that. I look around, wondering if anyone will come around the corner. I fall euphorically against the block wall.

The reprieve from reality is nearly immediate. I am free. Here and now, my crack is all that matters. I know I will never see the hardware store again. I am at home on these streets. This is where I belong.

The Streets

It's been weeks now since I've been living on the streets. David is showing me the ropes. He shows me the safest place to sleep in the park. It seems we will need to be looking for squat houses in a couple of weeks, when the cold weather sets in. He also leads me to the best Dumpsters to eat from. When we just want a break, we go eat some meals at the homeless youth shelter, but not often because we prefer the freedom of the streets. Sometimes we beg for change, but most of the time David just "does his thing" and brings back some cash.

"Give me a hit!" David demands.

"I'm out!"

"What the hell? What did you do with the rest?"

"Don't blame me! I have paid for all our fun!" I am annoyed.

"We need money. Quit fighting with me. Let's find some cash," I say with the conviction and paranoia of a crack fiend.

In my mind, all I can think is that "this kid" needs to go hustle some cash. I don't care what it takes. *He's just a faggot anyway*, I think. He did trick himself out to men on the block. While he never said that's what he was doing—I knew. I see these guys staring at him, older guys who look out of place on the streets. David sees them looking, walks over, and they leave together. Within about thirty minutes, David is back with cash. I don't ask, and he doesn't share. It seems strange—he's the same kind of faggot I would have kicked the shit out of in my younger years. But we need cash. We hustle. We do what it takes to survive.

"Did you have any luck?" I ask.

"Nah," he says.

"What about him?"

"Who?"

"Him, right there," I say as I point to a burly, brown-haired man. He has been staring at us since we started our discussion.

"It's worth a try." David shrugs as he heads across the street.

I never ask David what is required of him during these transactions. I don't want to know. *He's a faggot*, I think again as I watch him from across the street. *How could he do it? How could he let them touch him? How could he touch them? Prostitution is way below me.* As my father's face appears in my mind, I feel disgusted. I see him yelling those words at me. My father has ingrained in me a total hatred for these people—and for myself.

"He's not interested in me."

"Why the hell not? He's been staring over here for ten minutes at least!"

David's voice lowers, and he says, "That's because he wants you."

"What?!"

"Chill, man!" he says firmly. "Just hear me out. This guy doesn't want sex."

"Why the hell is he here if he doesn't want sex? Is he trolling the prostitution district looking for a good deli?"

"Nah, man, he's got a fetish," David says without emotion.

"A fetish? And what kind of donkey show is this john looking for?"

"Listen, this dude has real money! And he wants you. So shut your mouth and listen to me." He looks angry. "I am not going to miss out on good money because you're being a bitch. Man up!"

"Screw you," I say under my breath.

"Go talk to him!"

I know he won't stop until I do, so instead of fighting, I walk briskly across the street; all the while, this guy is just staring at me. Well, actually he is staring at my legs.

"Hey," he says sheepishly.

"Hi, man. My friend said that you wanted to talk to me."

"I have money," he states bluntly. "I am just going to lay my cards on the table. I have been staring at your feet, your boots, for the last fifteen minutes. I will pay you eighty dollars cash if you go into this parlor with me and let me lick them." He points at the sex parlor behind us.

"No sex?"

"No sex," he says firmly.

I follow him across the road with trepidation, keeping my eyes glued to the red "Sex and Peep Show" sign we are headed toward. *Am I really doing this?* I think. We walk through the front door, he gives the man what looks like a twenty, and we are escorted to a room. This room is no more than 8 feet by 8 feet. There is a bench along the back wall that substitutes for a bed, and on top of it is a thin mattress, if you could call it that. On the other end of the room is a sink.

I think, *I need to wash my feet.* I blurt out, "I need to wash my feet."

"Nooo!" he yells.

That stuns me. Why is he yelling?

"I'm sorry," he says. "It's just that, well, I get more turned on when feet are unwashed."

"Oh," falls off my lips with surprise.

"Take off your shoes and socks." As he says this, he begins to unbutton his pants.

The next thing I know, I'm laughing. I mean, this guy is licking my feet. *Really? What the heck am I supposed to do? Faggots are sick!* My mind is flooded with thoughts.

"Stop it now, or I won't pay you!" he grunts.

"Sorry," I say. David and I need the cash.

They say that you never forget your first time. This john will undoubtedly live in my memory—my first. *I know I can do this. This is much easier than when I was a child. I need to survive.*

I take his eighty dollars, which is the least valuable thing I have gained from this experience. Now it's all changed, and it's my turn to bring in some cash.

"Where's the doctor? I need to get our crack prescription refilled!"

"Woot, woot! Yes, Doctor Rich! Let's get that prescription filled!" David jokes.

We are two guys, taking back our lives one high at a time, as the clock "tricks" away.

When the End Begins

"Hey, Ma. It's Rich."

"Honey, I can hardly hear you. Where are you?"

"I'm alive. Just needed to hear your voice," I say. With this confession, a tear trickles down my face. Maybe I'm not as dead inside as I think I am.

"You there? I can hardly hear you."

"Sorry, Mom, I'm outside of the bus station. I just wanted to hear your voice."

"Grandma's dying."

The phone falls from my ear. I remember my little red truck, my grandma, the love. As I pull my phone up to my ear, I hear my mother in the distance.

". . . [O]ne week to live, but she could likely die in the next twenty-four hours. Please come home, Rich. Please."

I can hear her pleading with me. "OK. Wire me the money. Tell Grandma to hold on 'til I get there." I hang up the phone before my mom finishes talking.

"David!" I shout.

"What? Why do you look sad?"

"I have money coming. Let's stop by Western Union, then get f'ed out of our minds." I wipe the tears from my face. Goodbye, Grandma. I will never see her again. I know this.

Tricky Situations

I remember watching the teardrops of blood run down my inner thigh. Fissures—often the result of anal sex.

Six foot three, blond hair, disheveled, he speaks to me with that stark accent of the French-speaking Canadians. I think, *That is the problem with crack. It makes it hard to focus and understand what's going on. What is going on?*

"How do you like it, baby?" I hear. *How does such a promising young man as me find himself here?*

As he sits four feet from me, I wait. This is part of the game. At some point, he will be wanton enough for the main attraction. *I just hope it isn't soon. This free crack is too much fun.*

The next few days blur together, as Mr. Boy Lover watches me, high as a kite, for days. *Is it wrong that I'd go through it again and again? Am I sick? I am not sick! I am powerful! I am seductive! Who are these men to feel that they can lord their power over me? I am the one in charge. I am the one who lures, and they—they are the ones who take the bait. Dumb faggots!*

I realize he is staring, just waiting for my euphoria to wear low enough. He wants me to remember and know what is happening. His eyes meet mine. I know that this glance is different. It is not the same glance I would see in the eyes of a new trick. This is the glance that is given before the attack. Some animals lure prey; others attack and overpower. Mr. Boy Lover is of the latter. And I know in this moment that my attempts to run would be futile. I scream. "Please, no!" I hold my hands out to keep him at bay. He approaches methodically and directly.

What happens next I'll live over and over again through the history of my mind. He grabs me by the hair and forces me over the desk, face down. The shock is already setting in, and my dissociative abilities, honed through years of ritualistic abuse, gives way to full-blown detachment—One... Two... Three... Four.... I feel the warm sensation of blood. The rest is a blur, but the humiliation fills me from head to toe. I drop to the floor as my bowels release.

That's when he does it. He already has all I am—my dignity, my identity, my power—and yet this sick pervert feels the need to go further. Perhaps he does it to show me who's boss—as if I don't know. He leans down slowly and deliberately, his gaze never leaving mine. Slowly he runs his hand through my shit and pauses, staring wildly at me. I look down. As I do, he caresses my face, from my forehead down to my chin, leaving a warm, watery trail dripping from the corner of my mouth. I slump my head down to the floor, devastated.

"Get out!" he shouts. I gather my pants quickly and stumble back to the streets to find David.

Eight Years on the Streets of NYC

This has been a good week. I was able to land a Sugar Daddy last Wednesday! He let me live at his place for the week, and I can tell he will invite me back again. There is nothing better than a Sugar Daddy, especially in the winter. I hate sleeping at the shelter. This is a nice reprieve. Last year's Sugar Daddy was one of the best—he was a chef, and he fed me crepes, soufflé, and gourmet sandwiches. It was amazing! I hope this new trick is a repeat customer. Who doesn't like free room and board? Well, I guess it's not totally free. But making his every wish and fantasy come true is a small price for a warm, food-filled home. Plus, I can use all my money from work during the day to buy more crack.

"Are you Rich?"

"Yes, what can I do you for?" No worries today.

"I was told you are the best," he says.

I wait to answer, pondering if this guy works for the NYC police. He is short and pudgy. I can't imagine that he does. "I am."

"How much?"

"For what you want—no condom—it'll be one hundred and twenty dollars," I say matter-of-factly.

"I'll supply the crack if you promise not to give me any trouble," he says, pulling out a bag of crack.

"I think we have a deal," I say, and I wink at him. This day is getting better and better. He hails a cab, and we both get in. As the cabby takes off, the comfort of the seat overtakes me, and my eyes gently shut.

My Last Trick

The bounce of the taxi suddenly awakens me. It's dark out. Looking at the cab's dashboard, I check the meter to realize that it says $182. "Where are we?" I ask my current john.

"We're here. Sorry the ride was so long, but I'm a private person. I don't want to do this anywhere that I can get caught."

He seems genuine, but I can't shake this feeling that something's not right. He grabs my hand and says, "Come on, I don't want anyone to see us." He hurries me toward a large older home that is obviously sectioned into apartments. We climb a fire-escape-looking ladder on the outside of the building to the second floor. He opens the door and ushers me in. "I need a hit."

He pulls a pipe from the cabinet next to the refrigerator, places a large rock of crack in the pipe, and looks at me. "Before we smoke, I want to set some ground rules. I need you to respect me. This will all be perfect if you promise not to cause me any trouble." With the pipe in his hand, he walks through the kitchen and into the living room. "Do you understand that I need you to respect me?"

"I hear you. Yeah, yeah, I'll respect you," I say. I give him the answer he wants to hear, but something seems off. *Why's this queer so hung up on respect?*

"Change in here," he says, and he returns to the kitchen. I put down my backpack and quickly take off my clothes. *Let's get this over with.* Something about this place bothers me—really bothers me.

"I pulled out my old massage table just for you, so lie down," he says.

"OK, whatever you want," I say as I lie on my stomach. *Something is off.*

He begins to massage my back, and before I know it, this queer's put a cloth around my neck and is trying to strangle me!

Frantically, pushing him away, I leap from the table and search the room for my belongings. *Where's my backpack? It has everything I own—passport, clothes—everything.*

Now I'm really frantic. "Give me my backpack! Where's my backpack, you queer?"

I run to the nearest room to look for my stuff, and that's when I hear them. There's someone else in the back room. Queer and I aren't alone.

Running back into the kitchen, I see an old T-shirt on the back of a chair. I grab it and dart out the door. "Help! Help!" I scream as I run naked into the road, still holding the T-shirt. A car barrels toward me in the dark. I stand in the middle of the road and wave my arms, jumping up and down. "Help! Please stop!"

The car pulls over. "Are you OK?" an older woman asks from inside her Buick.

"Please help! Call the police," I say. I don't know if she understands the frantic mess coming out of my mouth, but she opens the passenger door, pulls out her cell phone, and calls the cops. I began to count in my head: One... Two... Three... Four....

The police arrive; I am huddled in the older woman's passenger seat, pantless.

"Sir, what's going on?" asks a female voice through the window. "Please step out of the car; here's a towel to cover yourself with."

I step out of the car. "He has my stuff, my license, my clothes!" I am almost shouting at her.

"Sir, you need to calm down. Who has your belongings?"

"The man that lives in that apartment." I point to the second floor of the old converted apartments.

"What is his name?"

"I don't know."

"You don't know?"

"No." I look at the ground, realizing how crazy I sound.

"Well, sir, I am going to go check with this man. You stay here with Officer Jenkins." She points to a second female cop who is with the driver of the car. "But I have to be honest. We may not be able to get your belongings back. We have no right to enter a personal residence. If this man does not corroborate your story, then you will have to be taken to a shelter or the hospital."

I look down. "I have to go with you when you talk to him. I think he will return my stuff if he sees me with you."

"Sir, this is against protocol. But there aren't many options, so I am going to let you come with me to talk to him. But I do not want you to enter the residence under any circumstance."

"Yes, ma'am." I walk toward the apartment, towel wrapped around my waist. I knock on the door.

My pudgy friend answers. "What the...what did I say about trouble?"

"Look behind me." I point at the police, who are twenty yards away. "Give me my shit, and all this goes away—just the fantasies of a paranoid crackhead."

He looks at me. He looks at the police. "Fine."

He returns quickly and hands me my bag. I open it quickly and take inventory. I hold out my hand.

He pulls out his wallet. "No more trouble." He hands me the money.

Park-Bench Clarity

It is unusually hot, I think while sitting on a park bench. It is the kind of day when you can feel your socks sticking to your feet. I laugh thinking of my first trick. That was almost ten years ago. I have been on the streets since.

I am not in the habit of rolling up my sleeves, but the weather requires it today. People amble to and fro past me down the walkway. And similarly, my mind wanders through the fog of the past decade: *"Faggot,"* Grandma, my truck, Mom, Father. I'm nothing. I'm a man who spent his whole youth seeking to attain life. But I have nothing to show for it. I am an empty shell of a man sitting on a park bench, slowly dying. *If I die*, I think, smiling, *I will finally be at peace.*

Inside, I am empty. Shallow. Unfulfilled. Dead. Shameful. And lost. I notice a man walking toward me from afar. He looks at me just like my first trick did. It is a look I have become all too familiar with. *I'm a junkie, my arms are covered with visible track marks, and I'm a mess*, I think. *What does he want with me?* I already know. He comes up to me, leans in, and whispers into my ear. I look up. Dazed. Confused.

He looks down. Intent. Unsatisfied. Desirously. "How much?"

I think, *I'm a junkie. I am a junkie! Don't you have a soul? Don't you see me as a person?*

He whispers again, a little louder, enunciating his words slowly. "How much?"

I can see he is getting annoyed. Good for him. I just sit enjoying my haze.

And slowly my lips form words. At first I don't realize what I am saying. I gaze opportunely into his lifeless eyes. We are both junkies. This guy is no more a "man" than I am. He is a junkie just like me. In the same way I want to get high off crack, he wants to get high off sex. I understand him; he understands me. That which he hates in me, I hate in him.

I don't know if I say all that's going through my mind out loud or just think it, but he turns and walks away.

Just like him, there's no fix that will truly satiate me.

I am done with this life.

Rehab

The pamphlet said this is the place. I look up at the front of the building. It says, "Providence Church."

"Hey, friend," a man says, extending his hand. "Your first time here?"

"Yes," I say nervously.

"My name is Mark. There's nothing to be afraid of." He smiles.

I don't know why, but I believe him.

Once inside, I meet some other people. Nothing new is being said. Mark stands up to speak. He starts. "Hi, my name is Mark, and I'm an addict."

I have heard this on TV before. I guess it really is like this.

He continues, "I used to be a male prostitute. I was addicted to drugs. I had sex to survive and to support my habit. When I was a kid, my dad was an addict. He beat me and my two sisters. His favorite pastime was calling me 'faggot....'"

What's that feeling? I think. I put my hand on my face. I'm covered in tears. I cry because I know this story. This is me. I keep sobbing for an hour. Mark walks over to me at the end of the meeting; my face is still red from tears. He grabs my hand. I slump.

"Sit up, Rich. You don't need to slump anymore."

"Will you help me?" my voice croaks.

"Yes," is his confident response. "What can I do to help?"

"Will you drive me to a rehab?"

As I walk out the door, I think of my grandma. I think about my truck, her love, my innocence. I wonder if I will be able to find what I have lost.

RICH'S VOICE

Looking Back

Perhaps a better family unit and better role models in my life could have steered me another way.

The only intervention I can see that would have helped me as a child when I was abused was if school therapists, teachers, and/or counselors got to the root of my behavioral problems (class clown, bullying other students, etc.) instead of labeling me as a "bad kid." I had so much sadness and pain built up inside with no outlet, so all of that pain turned to anger, and the walls went up. I guess this is typical for boys who have been abused, from others I've spoken to.

In my teen years, the path that I chose may have been altered if I had known that there were others like me who also had been abused and had issues with their sexuality. Knowing that I wasn't alone might have eased my mind when I was thinking that I was "the only one who is going through this," which made me feel like a freak and fueled my drug addiction and the behaviors that followed. More open support in the school system might have helped.

Maintaining Freedom

Staying away from people, places, and things associated with that life, and abstaining from drugs and alcohol help me maintain my freedom. I deal with my feelings today.

Understanding the psychology of men who pay for sex helped me forgive these men somewhat, although in some instances, I still have strong resentment. Resentment is like poison. When it comes up, I try to let it go to keep my sanity. Anger can often put me in a negative place, and I refuse to have my emotions controlled by my past anymore.

The loving support from a twelve-step program is what gave me a foundation to build a life. My best friends, Jimmy and Tom, and my sponsor, Mark, have given me unconditional love and support for more than a decade and continue not only to be in my corner, but also to serve on the board at Project Weber, the nonprofit organization I created.

My mother also is my hero. Paralyzed from the waist down at nineteen and confined to a wheelchair since, she is truly one of the strongest people I have ever known.

Prevention

It's hard for me to give direct advice because I didn't listen to it when I was a kid. I can only share my experiences. Since I was very young, I was warned of the dangers of drugs, prostitution, and disease. I chose not to listen because I didn't value my life. Only now do I find its value from surviving through the pain and horrors of the life I lived. I had to experience the darkness before I could appreciate the light. Hopefully, just reading this book and the testimonies in it will be enough to cause people to see things from another perspective.

Victims are often lured by a friend or an acquaintance at the direction of a trafficker.

Chapter 6

RECRUITMENT TACTICS

WHILE EACH OF THE five stories in this book gives a unique picture of the recruitment process, they have one common denominator— every survivor was lured by someone he or she knew. It is common for victims to be lured by a friend or acquaintance, with large numbers being recruited by same-sex peers at the direction of a trafficker.[1]

> *"We are finding that in 60 to 70 percent of cases, the victim knows the person who is trafficking them."*
>
> —Minneapolis police Sgt. Grant Snyder[2]

"Skip parties" are common recruiting grounds for teenagers. "Skips," a term coined by kids, are parties held during school hours in which youth are encouraged to skip school and bring a friend. Drugs and alcohol are provided freely, with the expectation that a girl will offer herself for sex at the party. If she declines, she can suffer gang rape and beating. The sexual encounters are typically visually recorded and used for blackmail purposes to keep the child from reporting the incident.[3]

Not only are teens recruiting their peers, but there is a growing trend of teenagers actually becoming traffickers. Law enforcement agencies are seeing pimps get started between the ages of eighteen and twenty, with some as young as sixteen. One study shows that the average age of men and women who begin pimping in Chicago is twenty-two, and they will stay in the "exploitation game" an average of fifteen years.[4]

> *"Kids are picking up kids and pimping them."*
>
> —New York City officer[5]

Recuiting Grounds

Traffickers, much like pedophiles, frequent locations where kids hang out in an effort to recruit them. The top-five recruitment sites are malls, bus stops, parks, playgrounds, and schools.[6] Other common locations are hallways of court buildings, fast-food restaurants, truck stops, youth shelters, and detention centers. A trafficker will often pay girls and boys a recruiting fee for luring unsuspecting kids out of youth shelters and into his hands.[7]

> *"A former Hopkins High School senior pleaded guilty Friday to prostituting one of her cheerleading teammates—a sixteen-year-old girl."*[8]

Technology and Exploitation

"Law enforcement officials across the United States have identified online sex ads as the number-one platform for the buying and selling of sex with children and young women."[9] Internet sites generated more than $45 million from sex ads from June 2012 to May 2013. Some of the popular technology platforms for recruiting youth are Facebook, Backpage, Eros, CityVibe, Myredbook, SmugMug, Instagram, Vine, and most other forms of social media that have an interactive property.[10] The Internet is, regrettably, a very effective tool for both traffickers and child predators. It provides a significant measure of anonymity to advertise, schedule, and purchase sexual encounters with minors.[11] One of the greatest challenges for law enforcement is identifying and locating victims solicited online. Traffickers use fictitious names, ages, and pictures of children to ensure they cannot be identified easily. "Ads that appear to be posted by an individual who is independently in the sex trade are often created by, or under the direction of, traffickers. As shown in Kate's story, traffickers often disguise themselves as the person in the ad when communicating with johns via the Internet, texts, or phone calls."[12]

"I was first forced into prostitution when I was eleven years old by a twenty-eight-year-old man. I am not an exception. The man who trafficked me sold so many girls my age, his house was called 'Daddy Day Care.' All day, other girls and I sat with our laptops, posting pictures and answering ads on Craigslist. He made $1,500 a night selling my body, dragging me to Los Angeles, Houston, Little Rock—and one trip to Las Vegas in the trunk of a car. I am seventeen now, and my childhood memories aren't of my family, going to middle school, or dancing at the prom. They are of making my own arrangements on Craigslist to be sold for sex and answering as many ads as possible for fear of beatings and ice-water baths."

—An openletter from M. C. to Craigslist[13]

Section 230 of the Communications Decency Act of 1996 grants Internet providers a measure of immunity from liability against child sex trafficking. The legislation states, "No provider or user of an interactive computer service shall be treated as the publisher or speaker of any information provided by another information content provider."

This legislation allows Internet providers to determine, voluntarily, the level of commitment they give to protecting America's children from sexual exploitation. Many advocates and government agencies are trying to pass legislation requiring Internet companies to impose an age-verification obligation on anyone who publishes online ads of a sexual nature.

"The court upheld immunity for a social networking site from negligence and gross negligence liability for failing to institute safety measures to protect minors—and failure to institute policies relating to age verification."

—Doe v. MySpace, 2008[14]

Gang Banging

"The list of groups involved in prostitution reads like a who's who of organized gang activity in the United States: the Bloods, Crips, Folk, Gangster Disciples, Latin Kings, MS-13, Starz Up, Sur-13, and Hells Angels."

—Attiyya Anthony, Journalist, crime reporter[15]

Gangs are expanding their activities to include child sex trafficking as a new source of income. Some gangs are diversifying their income by reducing or eliminating drug trafficking activities in favor of child prostitution, believing it is less risky to prostitute girls than deal drugs.[16] Girls who join male-dominated gangs are at high risk for sexual exploitation. They are often required to complete an initiation process called "sexing in," whereby they must provide sexual services for one or more of the established gang members.[17]

"Once there, the victims were instructed to walk through apartment complexes, going door-to-door to solicit customers while accompanied by a male bodyguard from the gang. The going rate for victims' services typically was thirty dollars to forty dollars for fifteen minutes of sex, and each victim often had sex with multiple men in one night (usually about five to ten customers) and over the course of multiple weekdays or weekends (including as much as seven days a week)."

—Court transcript, US v. Michael Tavon Jeffries[18]

Grooming

"These walls are funny. First you hate 'em, then you get used to 'em. Enough time passes, you get so you depend on them."
—Quote from *The Shawshank Redemption*[19]

The process of "grooming" or "seasoning" is the systematic destruction of a girl's will, independence, and identity. Its primary aim is to control her both physically and emotionally through a combination of physical, mental, and emotional abuses. Grooming can include any or all of these abuses:[20]

- Beating: With hands, feet, or objects
- Burning: Branding, cigarettes, lighters, or blowtorches
- Sexual assault: Rape or gang rape
- Confinement: Being locked in closets, trunks, or other tight spaces
- Deprivation: Of food, sleep, or even the ability to urinate/defecate without permission
- Emotional abuse: Verbal threats or brainwashing
- Isolation: Relocation, separation from family and friends
- Renaming: Giving the woman an online name or a stage name or calling her "bitch"

Several years ago, I spent time with a young woman who for many years had been called only "bitch" by her pimp and the other girls. She had grown so accustomed to the moniker that when she was free from exploitation, it took her a while to respond when someone called her by her given name. During her time of captivity she had lost a significant part of her identity, her name.

The longer a victim is in the hands of a trafficker, the further she is removed from her true identity. It is especially important to rescue a trafficking victim within the first six to eight weeks of enslavement, known as the grooming period. During this short period of time, she likely will still be in a state of crisis and will not have bonded with her trafficker. If she can be rescued before trauma bonding sets in, her ability to cope and process the trauma will be significantly easier and quicker.[21]

> *"At first it was terrifying, and then you just kind of become numb to it."*
>
> —Survivor[22]

The US Department of Justice indicates that traffickers accelerate the grooming process by introducing a child to various forms of pornography. She will be shown suggestive images, nudity, and progressively more graphic and violent sexual interactions. This process is to desensitize her to sexual activity between adults and children and to normalize deviant and violent sexual activities.[23]

Tattoos and Branding

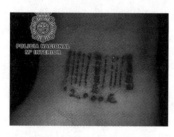

Barcode tattooed on trafficking victim. Spanish National Police

Traffickers often tattoo or brand their victims to demonstrate ownership and control. The tattoo or brand typically will be located on the child's neck, chest, back, legs, and sometimes the pubic area. Tattoos might be the trafficker's name or nickname, money related symbols, sexually explicit designs, and/or slang from the sex industry.[24]

Brands are typically made from coat hangers formed into a symbol or ornamental pattern. The brand is then heated or put under extreme cold and pressed into the child's skin to form a permanent scar.

"Taz, a sixteen-year-old girl here in New York City, told me that her pimp had branded three other girls with tattoos bearing his name. When she refused the tattoo, she said, he held her down and carved his name on her back with a safety pin."

—Reported by Nicholas Kristof, journalist, *The New York Times*[25]

Pimps not only like to tattoo their victims, but also themselves, as a way to flaunt their power and control over others. Several years ago, I met a young pimp in front of a Target store. He had a large tattoo across his neck that read "MOB." To his surprise, I walked up and asked him what it stood for. He smiled broadly and said, "Money over bitches." I smiled back and said, "Well, when you meet the right girl, you'll have to change that to BOM." He gave me a surprised look and laughed. I walked on—there was nothing more to say, and certainly nothing I could prove.

Pimps, Rates, and Quotas

"You charge him whatever you want to charge him; you ask if he's police or a pimp. He's gonna give you money, and then you're gonna just do whatever he wants you to do real quick. It's just a one-minute thing."

—Romeo, pimp[26]

There is a "method to their madness." Most pimps follow a relatively standard protocol within the pimping culture, as follows:[27]

- Most pimps manage only one to three girls at a time.
- Fifty percent of the pimps operate at a local level.
- One-quarter of the pimps are tied into citywide crime rings.
- About 15 percent of the pimps are tied into regional or nationwide networks.

- Ten percent of pimps in the United States are tied into international sex crime networks.

Typical rates in Ohio for street-level trafficking victims are as follows:

- Oral sex: $50
- Vaginal sex: $100
- Anal sex: $150

"Any man can kill, right? Any woman can be turned out."

—Sir Captain, pimp[28]

Another common practice is the enforcement of a nightly quota. This is the amount of cash a girl must earn before she is allowed to return "home" for the night. A quota typically falls in the range of $500 to $1,000 a night. If the quota is not met, a girl could be beaten, forced to return to the street, or deprived of sleep and food as punishment. The quota is non-negotiable, and she is to secure that amount of cash by any means necessary.

A recent prostitution sting turned up a surprising new trend regarding quota requirements in Oakland, California. If a girl has not met her nightly quota, she might be forced to set up a john so her pimp can steal his wallet, money out of the ATM, and in some cases, even his car. Brazenly, these pimps then sell the stolen goods to other johns.[29]

"Polaris Project, a Washington, DC-based nonprofit working with victims of human trafficking, recently conducted an informal analysis of a pimp's wages, based on direct client accounts. One teenage girl was forced to meet quotas of $500/night, seven days a week, and gave the money to her trafficker each night. This particular pimp also controlled three other women. Based on these numbers, Polaris Project estimates that the pimp made $632,000 in one year from four young women and girls."[30]

The recruitment tactics of traffickers are as diverse as the traffickers themselves. There is no one method that works on every girl, every time. This is why pimps are forever "changing the game," using the latest technology and incentives to lure the next generation of victims.

There Is Hope

"'You know what I just realized? All my life I have lived in chaos and drama. I was always fighting with somebody. I just realized now that I don't live in chaos; I'm trying to create it. But really I can just go outside and read a book!' I'm not sure if these words brought more joy to this fourteen-year old girl or to the staff in the group home she was living in. But that moment helped redefine 'normal' for this young lady. Over time she was able to allow herself to receive positive attention, began getting straight A's in school, participated in the therapeutic process, and eventually reunified with her mother. She now gets to create new memories—ones that end much happier!"

—Melissa Hermann, executive director, Courage House

The Inside Story

Samantha's story reads like a "textbook" by most child exploitation standards. She had a history of sexual abuse, was "set up" by a friend, and became addicted to alcohol and drugs to cope with the pain. What is unusual about Samantha's story is that she returned to the "life"—after being rescued.

For several years, Samantha has been a powerful spokesperson in the fight against child sexual exploitation. While this season of "speaking out" has been important for her healing process, Samantha has decided that this book will be the last time she shares her testimony for a while. She sees this book as a final chapter in her life as an "out-front" advocate and is eager to embrace the next phase of her life as a "behind-the-scenes" champion.

THE SETUP
By Stephanie Patterson

"What about this one?" Karen spins around and out of her closet, wearing a pink Op T-shirt that shows off her stomach. It is the third top she has tried on, and it looks good. She always looks good.

"I like it!"

"OK, then I'm done. But what about you, Sam? We've got to get you lookin' good for the high school guys," she says as she pulls a couple of shirts from her closet. I pull off my polo and slip into the first choice from Karen's pile. It's perfect! I straighten out the wrinkles of the purple blouse in the mirror as I admire how the color looks against my olive skin, dark hair, and brown eyes.

"You look great, Sam. Now let's get going. This is gonna be fun!" We scramble out the front door and into the backseat of her brother's Grand Am.

Karen and I are best friends. We met a year ago in the cafeteria on the first day of school. She's thirteen and a year ahead of me in the eighth grade, but we hit it right off and since then have been pretty much inseparable. Well, that is, except for the times when Momma catches us together and grounds me. Momma doesn't like Karen one bit. She calls her and her family bad blood and tells me to stay away from her. In some ways, she's right. Karen's mom drinks so much she can't hold a steady job, and her brothers are regularly getting in trouble with the cops. But with Momma working and Nolan, my stepdad, back in prison for another DUI, being at Karen's is way better than being at home alone. Besides, I dropped off the swim team the year before when I was late to practice one too many times. Momma never seemed to be able to get me there on time. So while my other school friends are going out for track or doing after-school choir, I'm at Karen's house hanging out with her brothers and whomever else happens to be around.

As we drive to the city, I roll down the window and let the wind blow through my hair. Karen's twin brothers, John and Marcus, both high school seniors, got an invitation to a house party in Kansas City, and rumor had it there were gonna be all kinds of drugs. When she heard that, Karen convinced them to let us tag along.

Karen and I have been smoking pot together since we met. It's part of our bond. We go out to the hill behind the school after class and smoke whatever we have. Karen is the main supplier, but she didn't introduce me to it; I'd already been smoking with my sisters for a year or so. She's just better at getting it.

John exits the freeway and turns into a neighborhood with tree-lined streets and nice-looking, two-story houses. He pulls up to a white house with blue trim. "This is it," he says as he leans over the backseat, "so remember what I said to you: Just play it cool, stick close to me, and I promise you, you'll get all the pot you want." We nod confidently as we slide out of the car.

Inside the house, loud music is blaring from the stereo, and people are everywhere. Some are dancing, and others are huddled in smaller groups smoking or snorting something. A few couples are making out on couches scattered around the room. John and Marcus push past the crowd and lead us to a dark room in the back of the house, away from the music and dancing.

"Stay here. We're gonna go grab some drinks from the kitchen and be back in a minute. Don't go anywhere else, OK?" John gives Karen and me a firm look. His eyes rest on Karen for a moment longer, and she nods. Karen and I look at each other, and then we realize we're not alone. A college-age guy with bloodshot blue eyes and shaggy blond hair is seated on a low couch. "Hi, girls. . . . Thanks for joining me."

Karen quickly befriends him. She is so friendly with guys. She always has a boyfriend or someone she's hanging out with. He offers us some pot, and we gladly accept, settling in to smoke our joints.

Karen has her arms around this stranger and is whispering something in his ear as I take my first puff. She catches my eye for a moment and winks ... and that's where the party ends in my memory.

When I come to, Karen and her new friend are gone, and I'm in an empty room staring up at a popcorn ceiling and a light bulb hanging by its wires. My head is pounding and fuzzy, and my body feels sore—like how I'd feel after an all-day swim meet. I push myself up to my elbows and take in the rest of the room. There are two boarded-up windows and a door with a hole where the doorknob once was. The walls are dingy, and the wood floor looks pretty beaten up. The mattress I'm on is the only furniture in the room, and outside of the small blanket at my feet, the mattress is bare. I lean over and see my pants in a pile on the floor. I don't know where my shoes are.* As I continue taking in my surroundings, my head starts to throb, and I let out a painful sigh. I'm pretty sure there was more in that joint than marijuana.

Just then the door opens and an arm slides in a plate with two sandwiches and a glass of milk. Seeing the food makes me realize I'm really hungry, and I overcome the headache enough to crawl to the food. I sit cross-legged eating the bologna and white-bread sandwiches and gulp down the glass of milk. I feel more clearheaded after the food and begin fiddling with the door, but it's somehow locked from the outside.

---

* Shoes: A victim's shoes are often confiscated to prevent her from running away.

"Hello!" I yell through the hole. "Can anyone hear me?" My voice echoes in the hallway.

I yell a couple more times and start getting scared—really scared. My mind runs away with thoughts of why someone would lock me up in a place like this. I try to figure out how I got here, but nothing comes together. The party feels like so long ago, and maybe it was. As the light fades outside, I'm overcome with a foreboding anxiety that feels very familiar.

That's when I hear footsteps in the hallway. They stop outside the door. I look through the hole, seeing nothing but jeans, and hear muffled voices. One set of footsteps walks away, but the jeans don't move.

I'm still cross-legged on the floor when he enters the room. I don't remember any details about him—the color of his hair or what he was wearing. All I remember is the look on his face. It was one I had seen on the face of my brother-in-law two years before. I shudder as the memory comes rushing back.

I had been over at my sister Amelia's house because Momma was running errands and wanted me out of her hair. It was OK because I liked Amelia. She asked me how school was going and what I was doing with friends, and she let me help her around the house. She also let me smoke with her, something I had come to look forward to. When we smoked, I felt more relaxed than I ever did at home. Amelia had married Sean about six months before, and they were already expecting a baby. She would let me put my hands on her belly and feel the baby kick.

When it was time to go home, I jumped in the truck with Sean for the short drive across town. We were about five minutes from my house when he pulled over into an empty parking lot and turned off the truck. He leaned across the seat and put his hand on my leg. "Don't worry. I'm not gonna hurt you," he said with a look on his face that made me nervous.

His hand moved up my leg and then under my shirt. I gasped and backed as far as I could toward the door.

"It's OK, Sam. ... Just trust me. You're gonna like this."

I couldn't believe what was happening. Sean had always been so nice to me, and now here he was—in an empty parking lot in broad daylight—touching me and having me touch him in places I had never seen.

The look on this stranger's face in front of me is the same look that was on Sean's face that day in the truck.

"Boy, they were right when they told me you were young," the stranger says. He smirks and squats down on the floor so he's at my level. "Come on. Come with me."

He lifts me up by the shoulders and leads me over to the mattress, and then he's on top of me, unbuckling his belt. He's old, maybe as old as my stepdad. I try to get away, but he pulls me back.

"Oh, no, you don't. You're staying right here with me, and you're gonna do exactly what I want. Understand?" His look hardens. He pulls off my clothes and then his own pants, then holds me down and has sex with me. I scream and twist in pain, but he doesn't seem to care. His body pounds against mine until he sighs and finally lets up. He lies with his dead weight on me for a moment before getting up and dressing.

"Bye, darlin'," he says as he leaves.

I lie on the bed until I hear the footsteps fade from the hallway and let out a single cry.

Before I can process anything, I hear footsteps again. I gather my purple blouse and pants, dress myself, and then scramble to the door to peer through. Again I see jeans and begin backing away in fear. The door opens, and a different man comes in.

The reality of what is happening hits me, and I shiver uncontrollably. I think back to the party and the last look I remember on Karen's face—the older guy she was with, the joint, how friendly she was with him—almost like she knew him from before. It all becomes a blur. I don't have the energy to fight this time, so I let him lead me to the mattress to do what he wants.

By the end of my first night in the room, the cycle has repeated over and over and over, with a different pair of jeans at the door every time. My body is sore, and my insides feel like they are burning. I want so badly to get up and take a drink of the water someone's left for me, but instead I fall into a restless sleep.

The next few weeks of my life consist of the same pattern. I sleep most of the day, eat what is given to me, and have men coming by all night. I have moments where I become clearheaded enough to try to figure out how I got here, but it's like my memory has been wiped clean from the time of the party to ending up in this room. I'm pretty sure my food is laced with some kind of drug because without the numbness I feel, the pain in my body would be too much to handle. But the drug doesn't numb the shame.

Two years ago, after Sean molested me, I got home and immediately called my older sister, Jamie, and her husband, Robert. I'm not one to keep things to myself. Despite being an alcoholic, Jamie still had the mother-hen mentality that came from being the firstborn. She was flaming mad when I told her what happened and sent Robert over to take me to the hospital. Meanwhile, she called the police and filed a report on Sean. They came to the hospital to question me and arrested Sean that night.

Robert sat in the waiting room with me, prayed for me, talked to the nurse, and took me home after the checkup.

When we got there, Momma was home, and she didn't want to hear anything of it. "You've got some nerve, Sam, sending a married man with a baby on the way to prison. Get to bed. You've got school tomorrow." I could see Robert's anger at her response, but he'd been dealing with

Momma's way of denying reality ever since marrying Jamie, and he'd given up fighting battles he couldn't win.

"Sam, I love you. Don't you forget it. You're precious," he said, kissing me on the head as he let himself out the front door. I didn't know it that night, but that would be one of the last times I'd ever see Robert. A few weeks later, Jamie had a bad drinking episode and ended up driving their car straight through the front of their house. They separated shortly afterward and got a divorce a few years later. He was one of the few men I ever felt truly loved me.

The day after Sean was arrested, I biked over to Amelia's to make sure she was OK. The door was open when I got there. I peeked in and saw her sitting on the couch, hands on her belly, crying. I knew it was because of what had happened, and I felt so ashamed and guilty—like I must have done something to have this happen to me. Sean had never, and then, I *must* have done something. I biked away without saying a thing.

The shame began that day I saw Amelia crying. And now, as I lie here trying to sleep after another night of men coming in, I can feel it growing inside me again.

I turn toward the door, looking for the glass of water that's waiting for me every morning, and that's when I realize the door is open. I'm up, dressing, and at the door in seconds. I pause to listen for a moment, but all I hear are the crickets outside. I tiptoe down a hallway, past a couple of other closed doors to a staircase that takes me into a big front room. The rest of the house is in about the same condition as my room: boarded-up windows, peeling paint, and a couple of torn-up pieces of furniture. I head for the front door, and I'm out.

Just like that.

I look back for a moment but see and hear nothing, so I make my way out to the sidewalk and start walking, then running, to a bigger road. I can't go as fast as I'd like because I still don't have my shoes, but I move as fast as I can without them. As I run, I pass houses that are in about the same shape as the one I came out of, with paint peeling and windows covered with black plastic. There's trash everywhere: on the sidewalks, in the gutter— everywhere. Most of the houses come right up to the sidewalk with no yard, just a metal fence. The cars are the nicest thing about this neighborhood. Most of them look brand new—like they just came from the car wash. Their paint sparkles, and they have gold and silver rims on the tires. As I head toward the intersection, I see a couple of black girls on the corner looking at me. They're wearing high heels and are dressed in spandex and shirts that show off their bellies. One of them is definitely wearing a wig because her hair is pinkish red. They're older than me, and the looks on their faces make me nervous. I turn to head the opposite direction, but just then a car comes around the corner. I jump out in the street to flag down the driver, hoping to hitch a ride home.

A man rolls down his window and says, "Can I help you?"

"Yeah, I need to get a ride out of here," I say, looking around nervously.

"Well, sure, honey. And what do you do?"

"Well, I just need to get home. I'll do anything to get home."

"Get in the car, then," he says and motions for me to jump in the backseat.

"Thank you, mister. I can't thank you enough. I—"

He reaches over the seat and grabs my arm. I'm scared, thinking I just got in the car of one of the guys who came to the house, and I go for the door.

"You're under arrest," he says as he pulls me back toward the middle of the seat.

"What?" I'm shocked.

"You're under arrest," he repeats as he clamps down on my arm.

"For what?" I say in disbelief.

"For prostitution. For soliciting me."

"Wh—what is that?" I ask. All I know about arrest is what happens to Nolan, my stepdad.

"Don't play dumb with me, girl. I see ones like you all the time."

"I just want to call my mom, please . . . ."

"Well, you can call her from booking at Juvenile Hall."

"What is that?" I ask again.

"You really *are* playin' dumb, aren't you? You got an early start, whore," he says.

"I—if you just let me call my mom, please," I beg him, but he's not listening.

"Mister," I try again, "I—I'm only twelve. I've been locked up in a house for days, with men coming all night. You've got to believe me."

"Well, things like that wouldn't happen if you stay out of this side of town," he says.

"Mister, I didn't get here on my own. They drugged me with something."

"Oh, don't act like you've never had drugs before. All you girls are up here for the same reason." He glares at me from the rearview mirror.

At that, I give up. This man is no more my friend than whoever had me locked up in the house. When we get to the jail, he books me and lets me call Momma. My hand is shaking as I pick up the phone. I realize I'm scared to death at what she's gonna say when she finds out I'm calling from Juvenile Hall.

"Hello?" It's Momma.

"Momma, it's me," I say weakly.

"Samantha! Oh, my God, where the hell are you?"

I don't want to answer her question.

"Momma, I'm here at the jail, but it's not what you think. I was at a party with Karen and—" She cuts me off. "It's the Juvenile Hall," I add weakly.

"OK. We're coming for you."

"Momma, wait.... I've gotta tell you what they did to me."

"Sam, we're on our way. We'll talk about it on the drive home," she says, and hangs up the phone.

The next thirty minutes creep by slowly. When she arrives, Nolan is with her. Momma looks at me, expressionless, then turns to the officer to go through some paperwork. Nolan grabs me by the shoulder and leads me out to the car. He is silent, but I can tell he's angry with me.

When Momma gets in, she wastes no time. "Samantha, I can't even tell you what the past two weeks have been like. The phone calls, the questions from people at work, the whole neighborhood. Hell, I've hardly been *able* to work dealing with all this. And how many times do I have to tell you I don't want you spending time with Karen? But what do you do? You go around me and do that very thing! Do you not hear me? I mean, what is your problem?"

I sit silently in the backseat. I don't even try to interrupt. She obviously doesn't want to hear what I have to say.

"Samantha, I was at the end of my rope before, but this. This is it, Samantha. I can't take it anymore. Only someone that's crazy does what you do, and I just cannot take it anymore. Now we're gonna get home, and we're gonna start lookin' for someone who can take care of you because I just can't do it."

I know what she means. Last year, when she caught Karen and me drinking, she threatened to send me to a Baptist home or boarding school.

"Now, Sam, I don't want nothin' of this talked about around the family or anyone else, you hear me? You've already disgraced me enough. No calling Robert or your dad or anyone." She glares at me, and I look away, tears streaming down my face.

When we pull into the driveway, I go to my room, crawl into bed, and fall asleep almost immediately. I feel like I could sleep for days, but at 6:00 p.m., Momma comes in and tells me to come to dinner.

"You need to eat and get back to bed because you're going to school tomorrow. Until we decide what we're gonna do with you, you're gonna keep going to school," she says decidedly.

"Are you serious? Momma, please, you have no idea how much pain my body—"

"That's enough! The decision is made. I won't have you staying around here and getting in more trouble."

When Momma found out about what happened with Sean, it was the same thing: go to school, don't shame me, stop finding trouble, and don't you dare talk about it. I guess I shouldn't have expected anything different this time.

So I never tell Momma about what happened in that house in Kansas City. Besides, I know she thinks it was me. She thinks I chose to go to that horrible house. I hear her talking about it on the phone with her friends. And Nolan, he hardly even looks at me anymore.

Later that week, I see Karen at school. I ask her about the party and she says, "You just disappeared and when I went lookin', you were gone. I figured you'd hooked up with some guy, and we had to go. So I just hoped you were OK."

Her explanation doesn't feel right, but I've stopped caring. I stop caring about a lot of things. And nobody ever asks me about anything. Nobody asks me how I feel. Nobody asks me why I'm not making good grades anymore. Nobody asks me why I don't want to do fun things. I cry myself to sleep every night, and during the day, all I want to do is get high to numb the pain.

About a year after escaping from the house, I'm really depressed. My grades have slipped so much that I am repeating the seventh grade, and I've stopped hanging out with all my friends. I spend most of my time at home alone, or with Karen—if I can sneak around Momma. I start contemplating suicide and even make a couple attempts by cutting my wrists with a dull razor blade I find in the garage.

After two trips to the emergency room, and subsequent groundings, Momma comes in my room one day and tells me she's found a place that can help me: St. John's, a mental institution. I know about it because at school we'd joke about people who ended up there.

"It's for the best, Sam. I can't take care of you anymore. You're too much for me, but St. John's has people who know how to deal with this kinda stuff. We're gonna leave on Friday at noon, so have your bags packed by then, and say your good-byes this week."

In a moment of desperation, I decide to try to contact Dad. The next day after school, I ride my bike to the pay phone at 7–Eleven with a handful of quarters. I haven't talked to my dad in years because after he got remarried, Momma got jealous, and her way of punishing him was not letting him see me anymore. I don't understand it because Momma had already married Nolan by that time. But that's just the way she is. Every year, Dad sends me a birthday card with twenty dollars in it and writes me a long letter all about his life and what he is doing. He's in construction, so he travels a lot for whatever job he's working on. My fourteenth birthday was a month ago, and his card came. This time it was sent from Chicago; he's there working on a new skyscraper.

I snuck two phone numbers for him from Momma's address book the night before. I wasn't sure which one was the most recent, so I took both. The first one goes straight to the operator saying it's no longer in service. I try the second one. It rings and rings and rings until finally someone picks up.

"Hello?" It's a woman's voice.

"Hey! This is Sam. I'm looking for Vernon. Is he home?"

"No. … I think you got the wrong number. There's no Vernon that lives here."

I'm crushed, "Are you sure? He's not just traveling?"

"No, hon, I'm sure. You've got the wrong number. I'm sorry." She must have heard the disappointment in my voice.

"OK. Well, thank you anyway."

I hang up the phone, slide down the wall of the phone booth, and cry until it hurts. I'm out of options. Robert and Jamie are going through their divorce, Amelia has her hands full with the baby, and now I can't even find my dad. What's left?

I bike to Karen's house and knock on the door. Karen answers.

"Hey, what do you say we get out of here?" I say.

"Get out of where?" she asks.

"Here. What do you say we get out of here and go to the city? I just found out my momma got me a place at St. John's. She's taking me there on Friday unless I figure something out on my own."

Karen raises her eyebrows. "Well, where ya wanna go, Sam? You know a place?"

"Well, not really. I mean, I was hoping you could help me figure that out. Or maybe your brothers know a place?"

"Let me talk to them and see what they say," she says, and a sly smile appears. Karen is always up for an adventure.

"Look," I say, "I gotta get home before Momma realizes I'm late from school. See you tomorrow?"

"Sounds good, Sam. I'll talk to them tonight," she says. I hop on my bike and pedal away.

The next day at school, Karen pulls me aside and tells me her brothers are going to the city for another party that night and will take us along. They've got a friend who will let us stay with him for a while and sell us joints for a dollar apiece. We make our plans to meet at Karen's house that night. Before leaving, I go into Momma's room and grab the forty dollars cash that's in her jewelry box. She's working the night shift, and Nolan is out drinking, so there is no one to suspect anything.

We get to the city, and John pulls his car to the curb. "OK, this is it."

Something about where we are feels familiar to me.

"See that house over there with the silver car out front?" John points to a house across the street. "That's Derek's place. You just tell him John sent you, and he'll take care of you."

"Perfect!" Karen says excitedly, "Bye, guys! We'll find our own ride home, so don't worry about us." We hop out of the car, and they pull away.

It's dark out, but under the streetlight I see two black girls, and then I realize what's so familiar. I turn to look behind me, and sure enough, there is the abandoned house where I was locked up. Karen doesn't notice I've stopped following her. For a few seconds I stand there frozen, with all kinds of thoughts running through my head. *Were Karen's brothers in on what happened to me, or is it just a fluke that they took us to the same place? Was Karen in on it? What do I do now? I was the one who wanted to get away. Do I tell her?*

I think back to the morning I escaped from the house—my hope when I saw the car pull to a stop, followed quickly by the cop's cruel words: "All you girls are up here for the same reason."

I guess he was right. Here I am, back for the drugs.

Karen is several steps ahead of me. "Sam? Are you all right? You look like you've seen a ghost."

"I'm good. I'm coming," I say.

I decide at that moment not to tell Karen about the house. As far as I can figure, there's no point in bringing it up. I don't want her to think I'm accusing her of being involved. As we walk down the block toward Derek's house, people are coming out on the streets. The girls are dressed in spandex, short shirts, wigs, and lots of makeup. They stand on their corner, two or three of them, mostly black girls, and the men with them stay within a couple hundred feet, keeping an eye on them.* They're all much older than us.

Everyone we walk past is staring at us, and they don't even try to hide it. The girls look suspicious, and some of the guys whistle, but Karen seems oblivious to the attention, so I just stay close to her. I don't have much of a plan beyond getting away from home, and I am feeling a little uneasy now about my decision. Thankfully, Karen has always been fearless.

We walk up to Derek's house, and Karen knocks on the door. A large black man answers. "Well, hello, ladies! How can I help you tonight?"

"We're looking for some pot, and my brother John said you'd take care of us," Karen says with confidence.

"Ah, you must be his sister, Karen. He told me you'd be coming. Have a seat."

He leads us to some dusty couches, and we each buy a joint for a dollar. After our first, we buy another. And then another. We start getting goofy and giggly and then really tired. Derek brings out some blankets and lets us sleep on his couches.

After a couple days of being in the neighborhood, I realize that most houses on the block are a lot like Derek's: some sell joints, others sell special types of alcohol, others are crack houses, and almost all of them are whorehouses.

It's been about a week now of Karen and me wandering around the neighborhood and spending our nights at Derek's when we run out of cash. So Karen says, "Come on, let's go see how the other girls make their money."

---

* Catcher: Usually a younger "wannabe pimp" who is paid by a pimp to watch his girls on the track to ensure that they are following the pimp's orders.

As night comes, we go out to the street and watch the other girls. Cars pull up with men in them, the girls get in the car, it pulls away, then after a while, they come back with money.

Both of us are smart enough to figure out what's going on. "OK, I'm gonna give it a try," Karen says as she takes her place on an open street corner. I hang back, closer to Derek's house.

It's not more than a few minutes before a car slows to a stop. Karen is the only blond-haired, blue-eyed girl on the street, and she is by far the youngest. I watch the car pull away with her inside.

For as long as I've known Karen, she has been bold with guys, and I know she's been having sex for a couple years now with her boyfriends. But getting in the car with a complete stranger is a whole different thing.

Not more than twenty minutes later, she's back, and sure enough, she has some cash. "That was easy," she says. "I'm gonna try it again."

She goes back to the corner, and the routine repeats itself. After she comes back from the second trip, one of the men who had been watching us from across the street starts walking toward us. He had come to Derek's a few times; his name is Tate. He's a tall guy, real skinny and lanky—which makes it look like he's always walking with a limp—and he's got tattoos all up and down his arms. The biggest one across the inside of his arm says "Daddy"*
in scroll-like letters. He flashes a smile at us, revealing his gold teeth. "Y'all have been staying with Derek, yeah? Why isn't he taking care of you?"

Karen answers, "Well, we ran out of money, so we just need to get some more, and then we're fine."

"If you like what Derek has, I can give you even better stuff, *and* I'll take care of you. I'll make sure you have a place to sleep and good clothes and food. You won't have to worry about anything. What do you say?"

---

* Daddy: The term victims are often required, or choose, to call their pimp.

Karen and I look at each other. "Give us a minute," I say.

"Sure, take your time. You know where I am," he says as he heads back across the street. There was something about the way Tate said "I'll take care of you" that gave me hope. If I was going to be doing this stuff, I wanted someone to protect me. I didn't want to end up in a situation like I did after the party.

"I think it's a good idea. What do you think?"

"I don't know," Karen says with hesitation. "Derek's been pretty cool letting us stay with him. If we just get some money, we'll be fine."

"But he's not gonna let us stay forever. He's got a business to keep up; he can't have us taking up his space all the time," I respond. "Besides, if we don't like it, we can always leave."

"All right, if you say so. I guess we can give it a try," she answers.

So Karen and I are now Tate's girls, and he is our "daddy." Tate's bottom girl gets me all dressed up, and I go out to the corner with her for my first night on the street. I'm a nervous wreck. My heart beats faster, and my palms get sweaty each time a car pulls up. The third car that night is a blue pickup truck. After talking to the driver, she says to me, "OK, this one's for you."

Every trick I turn that first night is scary, but after about a week of being trained by Tate's girl, it's no big deal. It's just what I do.

We work the streets at night and sleep most of the day. And Tate keeps his word. We give him our money, and he gives us whatever we want: drugs, clothes, shoes, and perfume. We are well taken care of.

Everything is going fine for a couple weeks, until one day when Tate is out of pot, and that's what we want.

"We're going to Derek's to get some pot," Karen says nonchalantly.

"Oh, no you're not. You're staying right here," he says.

"Whatever. You said you'd always have it, and you don't, so we're going over there. We'll be back in a bit," she answers.

He slaps Karen hard, and she falls to the ground, holding her cheek. "You're not going anywhere. You're *my* bitches[*] now, you got that? So you do what I say." He walks off, leaving us in our room.

That night, Karen makes plans to leave. While Tate is getting dinner, she sneaks off to Derek's to call John and arrange for him to pick her up. She tries to convince me to go with her, but where do I have to go? As crazy as her family is, at least she has a home to go back to. But Momma, she'll take me straight to St. John's. I know it.

So I stay, and working the streets becomes my life. Every day is the same routine. We get up at 5:00 p.m. and prepare for the evening. Tate likes to keep things fresh, so we have a huge closet full of stuff to choose from: all kinds of wigs, jewelry, spandex pants in all colors, and midriff tops. We get dressed for the night and then have hamburgers or fried chicken for dinner at a place a few blocks away. We work all night until the sun comes up. We bring Tate all the money we earn, and in exchange he gives us whatever drugs we want. I'm Tate's favorite girl because I'm the youngest. He takes extra good care of me—especially now that Karen is gone. His lead girl coaches me to tell people I'm only eleven because, as she says, "They're always lookin' for a younger one."

After almost a year of working for Tate, I'm out on my corner one night and see a brown sedan coming down the block. There's something familiar about the car, but it doesn't click for me until it's too late. The car speeds quickly toward me, pulling up on the curb. It's Momma.

"Sam! Get in the car!" She jumps out and starts pushing me toward the car. I resist, but she overpowers me and pushes me in the backseat. We speed off in the direction of the expressway, and the monologue begins

---

[*] Bitch: A term used by pimps, prostitutes/victims, and customers to address or refer to a victim.

with her rattling on about how angry she is. I realize we're not headed in the direction of home, so I ask where we're going.

Momma rolls her eyes, "Like I have to tell you, Sam. We're going to St. John's."

When we arrive, two men come to the car to get me. Momma comes in, too, but goes the opposite direction into a small office. The men lead me down a long hallway and into a small room with two chairs and a table. I wait alone for half an hour until Momma arrives with an older man wearing a white doctor's jacket and carrying a clipboard. He sits down at the table with me, but Momma remains standing.

"Hello, Samantha," he says, "I'm Dr. Crawford. I've been speaking with your mother, and now I'd like to ask you a couple of questions."

I nod.

"Your mother has stated that you have exhibited unstable behavior, putting yourself in dangerous situations and threatening to take your own life. Is that right?"

I answer Dr. Crawford, "Well, when you have to live with someone like her, you'd feel the same way," I say, avoiding eye contact with Momma.

"Well, then, Samantha, we'd like to see if we can help you. You're going to be staying with us for a while. I'm going to give you a moment alone to say good-bye to your mother," he says as he gets up and leaves the room.

I glare at her with my arms folded across my chest.

"Samantha, these people are equipped to take care of you much better than I am," she says firmly. She kisses me on the forehead and then turns for the door.

"Thanks for nothing!" I scream after her. I pick up my chair and throw it at the door and am going for the next one when the two men come in and pin me down. One of them has a syringe, which he sticks in my arm. I collapse to the floor almost immediately.

I wake hours later in a room on a twin bed. There's a bookshelf and a chair in the corner, and light streams in through a small window. There's a knock at the door, followed quickly by a man entering with a glass of water and a plate of food. He sets it on the bookshelf, gives me a quick look, and leaves.

So here I am again: drugged and locked in a room with people leaving me food and water. Only this time they say it's because they're going to help me.

I spend the next three years of my life at St. John's. Dr. Crawford diagnoses me as bipolar and paranoid schizophrenic and gives me drugs to treat my sickness. Eventually, they move me into a room with three other women. I make a few friends and pass the time by reading romance novels. When my eighteenth birthday is within six months, Momma starts visiting more often to convince me to stay willingly until I'm well, but I've already decided that won't be the case.

A few days before my eighteenth birthday, she tries to convince me one last time. Dr. Crawford shows me into the visiting room, and I can tell Momma's clearly upset about something.

"Samantha, your mother has something to tell you, but she's having a hard time with it," Dr. Crawford says as he coaxes me into a chair.

"Well, of course she's got something to tell me. She's never short on words," I say with a mocking tone. Our relationship has not progressed at all from where we were three years ago. I'm surprised when she stays serious, eyes fixed on her feet. "Samantha, you need to know something important about your father."

Now she has my attention. "What is it? Is he OK?"

"Yes, yes. Vernon is fine. But what I need to tell you is that Vernon... he's not your real father."

I sit there stunned. Vernon. Dad. I'm even named after his mom.

"You're lying! You're a liar! You're a lying bitch; you always have been!" I'm screaming at the top of my lungs while attempting to control the tears that are streaming down my face. "Give me the phone! I'm calling him."

"Samantha, I don't think that's a good idea. I knew I should have told you before, but I could never find the right time, and he didn't want me to tell you, either. But you're an adult now, and you need to know the truth." She continues to rattle on, but I'm ignoring her.

I step out of the room and into Dr. Crawford's office to call my dad. He must have known this would be my response because he already has the receiver ready to hand to me. Dr. Crawford dials Dad's number, and after two rings, he picks up. "Hello?"

"Dad, it's me," I say, attempting to control my shaky voice.

"Well, hey there, Sam, it's good—"

I cut him off. "Dad, Mom just showed up here at St. John's tellin' me that you're not my dad. And I just can't believe the nerve of her—right before I'm ready to go. It's like she doesn't care, making up these lies about you. She's never cared about anyone but herself, Dad. Can you believe this?"

I pause for a moment to give him a chance to agree with me, but he doesn't respond. Instead, I hear him crying on the other end of the phone and realize Momma's not lying. I hang up the phone without saying good-bye and storm out of Dr. Crawford's office, back in the direction of my room. Momma runs after me, explaining how they were just trying to protect me, but I block her out. I slam the door to my room and bury my face in my pillow. If I thought I felt alone before, it was nothing compared to what I feel now: Those who I thought were my family my whole life aren't even related to me.

Five days later, I'm released. I'm given some money for my bus ticket home, but instead I hitch a ride with a stranger headed for Oklahoma. I'm quiet in the backseat, wondering what to do next as the dreams of starting over and getting an education or meeting a good man and having my own family someday slip away. Everything I've ever cared about or hoped for feels like it has been taken from me.

The stranger takes me as far as a truck stop on the Missouri-Oklahoma border, and I hop out, thanking him for the ride. Within days, I've returned to prostitution. I'm the new girl at the truck stop. I hear the guys talking about me; they call me the "lot lizard."[1] I have a steady stream of clients and don't really need a place to live since I sleep in a different man's truck cab every night. Most of the ones who do drugs share what they have, so before I know it I'm back on the pot, and occasionally cocaine, when I get lucky.

Thus begins the next twenty years of my life. I go from prostituting at truck stops to ending up on a ranch in east Texas as part of a drug trafficking ring, and ultimately back in Kansas City, working out of a crack motel. I am in and out of prison the entire time, but whenever I get out, I always find my way back to my little motel, taking on clients as needed to support my addiction. My drug has become my pimp.

By the time I hit my late thirties, I've been in and out of prison more times than I can count, and I'm tired. I'm alone in my room one night, higher than a kite after finding out Vernon has died. I catch my reflection in the mirror and pause, as if seeing myself for the first time in ages. My face is bony. Wrinkles have formed around my eyes, and my mouth droops down in a constant frown. My skin is gray, and my eyes are hollow. But then there's my chestnut hair. Momma always said it was my best feature, and somehow it still picks up the shine from the light overhead, like the women in the shampoo commercials. Suddenly, I want nothing to do with it, and I root around in the closet until I find a pair of rusty scissors. I begin to chop off my hair, grabbing chunks at a time and working through them with the dull blades. With every handful of hair that falls to the floor, it's as if I'm accepting the loss of all I've never had. Vernon is dead. My family is not my family. I have no goals. No values. No morals. No purpose. I prostitute myself for drugs and live from trip to trip. I finish the haircut, my eyes blurry with tears as I curl up in a ball on the floor and fall asleep.

I wake the next day, surprisingly clearheaded and sober for the amount of drugs I took. I feel the coolness of the linoleum floor against my cheek, my eyes focusing on the chunks of hair and small bits of dust in front of me as the morning sun filters through the window.

I roll to my back and look up at the ceiling, breathing deeply. Something feels different. I go to the mirror to survey the damage of my haircut and laugh at the messy, uneven bob I've given myself. I feel the weightlessness of the hair that is gone, but more than that, the weightlessness of my soul. It's like I have finally allowed myself to grieve, and it has left me empty—like a glass ready to be filled.

I've had other moments through the years—and especially the past six months—when I have wanted to change. But deep-rooted shame from how I had lived my life always dragged me back down into the very things I was trying to escape. But today feels different. I reach into my pocket and pull out a business card that reads, "Hope for Recovery." I found it in the lobby a few months ago and have been carrying it around in my pocket ever since. I walk across the room to the telephone and pick up the receiver. My hands are shaking as I dial. I hear the ring on the other end of the phone and say to myself out loud, "Samantha, today is the day."

SAMANTHA'S VOICE

Prevention

My vulnerability to being trafficked began when I was ten years old. Being molested by my uncle was a horrific and scarring experience, and the lack of counsel and care from my family—or anyone, for that matter—left me damaged and wounded. I remember having nightmares for months in which I would see my uncle and other men violate me. I would wake up in a cold sweat, breathing hard and scared stiff, but I honestly didn't feel like there was anyone I could talk to about it. We were going to church sporadically, so I did not have close relationships with anyone there, and I didn't have a connection with any of my teachers or counselors.

What I did have was access to drugs, and while they did not help me process what had happened, they did numb the pain.

When I was arrested after escaping the house where I was held captive is another moment when I believe intervention would have changed the trajectory of my life. As a twelve-year-old victim of sex trafficking, I was treated like a criminal. It sounds atrocious, but it still happens today, decades later. Legal protocol is just now being developed for how to identify and handle child victims of sex trafficking. As a result, many victimized children are treated as delinquents when brought in on charges of solicitation.

My time at St. John's was intended to be an opportunity to get away from all negative influences and start over, but it did not serve me well. While I don't think medicating is always wrong, in my case it only reinforced my dependency on drugs. Counseling and group sessions were involved in my treatment, but the drugs enabled me to fake my way through it all without ever confronting the real issues.

Maintaining Freedom

For me, friendship is a cornerstone of the freedom I have today. Pearl—my sponsor through AA—is an incredible woman. She can see right through me and doesn't pull any punches. But she does so in the most graceful and loving way. Pearl has experienced a lot of pain and betrayal in her life and has overcome it. She has learned to forgive and start again. Pearl was the first person I ever met who really, truly believed in me. She led me through the Twelve Steps, and she has never once given up on me, even when I wanted to give up on myself. I don't think I ever experienced unconditional love until I met Pearl. She is the mother I never had, and having her in my life has brought tremendous healing.

Finding deep relationships has gone hand in hand with finding faith. I have a wonderful church community that has helped me through the highs and lows of the past several years.

Going back to school is another important part of rebuilding my life. The challenge and discipline of learning has helped me stay focused. It's been hard—really hard—and I have not yet completed my degree, but it is my most sincere hope that once I graduate, I can use what I am learning to help other people, especially children, who are in situations like I was.

The truth is, staying free is something I have to work at every day. There are constantly things that remind me of how far I have to go. Getting married was a huge step for me and something I had always dreamed of. When we got divorced a few years later, it was a really low moment and probably the closest I have ever been to returning to my old lifestyle. I slipped into a deep depression, and there were entire weeks when I didn't get out of bed. I was fighting suicidal thoughts, and had it not been for Pearl and a few other close friends, I don't think I would be alive today.

The hardest thing for me to do is accept where I am in the healing process on a daily basis and be OK with it. If I'm having a bad day, it means learning to give myself grace and not beat myself up for taking a step or two backward. My mind will tell me that I should be further along than I am, that other people think I should be further along. It is when I compare my progress to some arbitrary standard that I find myself struggling with depression and hopelessness.

I have had the privilege of speaking at churches, schools, and conferences about the dangers of sex trafficking and drug use. While I love the opportunity to help others through sharing my story, there can be the added pressure of wondering if I'm good enough, healed enough, removed enough from my past to be worthy of sharing my story. My mind can use this against me.

Words To the Wise

While my story is unique, there are common themes that repeat themselves in the stories of so many other victims of trafficking.

The first is that trafficking is often connected to drug use. Whether drugs are used to kidnap the victim or to build an addiction that causes the victim to choose to stay willingly, they are frequently an integral part of the lifestyle. In my case, my early exposure to drugs led me to put myself at risk willingly. In the end, it kept me bound to a lifestyle of prostitution.

My friendship with Karen is another commonality between my story and others'. Karen was my best friend, and quite honestly one of my only friends. I didn't want to accept that she and her brothers were involved in my being trafficked. I chose to remain oblivious and continued to go behind my mother's back to spend time with Karen.

And finally, shame is the common emotion I share with so many other trafficking survivors. I let the false responsibility of those things I had been victim to define who I was, so much so that I began hurting myself. I was my own worst enemy and a victim at the same time. If I could have a conversation with twelve-year-old Samantha, I would say one word: forgive. Forgive Sean for molesting you, forgive Momma for being angry and controlling, and most of all, forgive yourself. Let go of the shame you're holding on to, and find the courage to look at your life with all its challenges and start fresh. Today is the day.

The majority of child kidnapping cases are at the hands of someone known by the child or family.

Chapter 7

KIDNAPPING

THERE IS A MISCONCEPTION about the prevalence of kidnapping in child sex trafficking occurrences in America. Fewer cases involve abduction than you might think.

Kidnapping Stats

A recent study from the Polaris Project confirms that only 11 percent of sex-trafficked women and children in the United States were abducted through force.[1] Most of us associate sex trafficking cases with the dramatic child abduction stories we see highlighted in the media, such as that of Elizabeth Smart, who was abducted from her bedroom window at age fourteen; or Steven Stayner, who was kidnapped at age seven while walking home from school.

Abduction-related trafficking cases typically differ from other child abduction cases in that the majority of trafficking cases involve some type of "setup." The setup is the initial luring of the victim under false pretenses. The "lurer" can be a known party, as in Samantha's case (which you just read) and Debbie's case (which follows), or it can be a stranger. Initially the setup likely will be nonconfrontational. However, once a victim recognizes the potential danger and attempts to leave, often she will be threatened with physical violence and forced to stay.

> *"One evening, Debbie said she got a call from a casual friend, Bianca, who asked to stop by Debbie's house. Wearing a pair of Sponge Bob pajamas, Debbie went outside to meet Bianca, who drove up in a Cadillac with two older men, Mark and Matthew. After a few minutes of visiting, Bianca said they were going to leave. ... Unbelievably, police say Debbie was kidnapped from her own driveway with her mother, Kersti, inside. Back home with her other kids, Kersti had no idea Debbie wasn't there."*

—ABC News[2]

The majority of trafficking- and nontrafficking-related kidnapping cases are at the hands of someone known to the child or the family. According to the US Department of Justice, Office of Juvenile Justice Delinquency Prevention Juvenile Justice Bulletin, June 2000, *"Based on the identity of the perpetrator, there are three distinct types of kidnapping: kidnapping by a relative of the victim or "family kidnapping" (49 percent), kidnapping by an acquaintance of the victim or "acquaintance kidnapping" (27 percent), and kidnapping by a stranger to the victim or "stranger kidnapping" (24 percent)."*[3]

Even with the best intentions, we cannot always protect our children, as the next story reveals. Being armed with the statistics that our children are more likely to be "set up" by a friend or acquaintance than a stranger gives us some powerful inside information. Knowing our kids' friends and acquaintances might prove to be the most beneficial approach to keeping them safe.

> *"If you know the enemy and know yourself, you need not fear the results of a hundred battles."*

—Sun Tzu[4]

There Is Hope

"It was in the rough part of town, and the brothel bouncer just glared at my petite blonde friend as she handed him her phone number. 'I am a counselor and would like to offer my number to any of the girls who want to talk,' she said. He glared silently until she almost walked away. Then she got up the courage to say, 'Please, please just give them my number.' He must have thought she was just spunky enough because he finally said, 'Just one card, if you want them to have your number? Don't you have more cards for me to give them?' With a deep sense of satisfaction, she gave him all of the cards she had. As he walked away, I knew that a door I had long been waiting for had slowly begun to open."

—Marie Watson, founder, Unending Hope

The Inside Story

The writers and I are committed to sharing each survivor's story with accuracy and integrity. With that in mind, each survivor has been given the opportunity to read and approve his or her own story. Deidra and her mom chose to read her story together. After reading the draft, Deidra's mom was startled to see how we depicted her as such a "helicopter mom," closely monitoring her daughter's whereabouts. When she asked Deidra if this was an accurate picture of her mothering style, Deidra replied, "They nailed you, Mom." They both had a good laugh, and the story was approved.

TAKING DESTINY
By Philipa A. Booyens

There's not much to do during spring break, especially when my mom's paranoia makes me feel like a prisoner. She won't let me out of her sight because of my mental development issues. I can't sense danger like most people do, so the class trip to Destin, Florida, is definitely out of the question.

It's April 2008, my senior year, and I'm stuck in the passenger seat of my mom's SRX with my little brother and sister in the back, screaming and hitting each other. "Mom! Make him stop!" Abby yells while Noah sticks his tongue out at her. I try unsuccessfully to ignore them.

"Cut it out already! We're almost home!" Mom shouts. I wonder if her overprotection is as tiring for her as it is for me.

Abby screams again, and I turn up the radio volume. "Summer Love" drowns out everything else as I stare at beautiful shopping centers and clean streets. Brentwood, one of middle Tennessee's nicest suburbs, is so boring this time of year. Thankfully, my phone vibrates, and I read the text.

Aaron: "Hey Deidra ur still here right?"

Me: "Yeh u?"

Aaron: "Yep wanna hang out?"

My thumbs pause as I look up at my mom. I'm afraid to ask, but she knows Aaron from my special ed classes, so this should be OK. He's into community service and from a devout Mormon family. They're supposed to be really good people—don't drink, don't party, that type of thing. That's probably why she had him over for dinner a few weeks ago, to make sure he was safe to hang out with.

Aaron: "Is it ur mom? Did I pass?"

Britney's "Piece of Me" plays on the radio now, only encouraging my frustration. I turn it down, even though Abby and Noah are still fighting when Mom pulls into our quiet subdivision. "Mom!" I yell over them. "Can I hang out with Aaron?"

"Mormon Aaron?" She doesn't look at me or wait for me to respond. "Only if he comes to our house and only until eight."

My irritation quickly fades into excitement. I text Aaron back as we park in the two-car garage. Greg, my stepdad, isn't home yet. My cell vibrates before I put up the groceries.

Aaron: "See u soon."

It's five by the time the doorbell rings. Noah chases Abby around the house, and Mom wrings her hands through her hair. She's right by me, though, when I open the door, reminding me that she's the warden of my prison.

"Hi, Aaron." She greets him with a forced smile.

The sandy-haired boy wears a blue and gold cap (our school colors), white polo shirt, and jeans. He shuffles and looks at the floor. For a small woman, my mom's pretty intimidating.

"Well, don't just stand there. Come in," she says. "Food's already on the table."

Abby screams again, and Mom runs off to check on her. Aaron follows me inside to the kitchen that smells like homemade lasagna and garlic bread. Greg's the only dad I've ever really had, so I'm thankful he's here to greet Aaron with a smile and handshake before getting seated. "Aaron, nice to see you again."

"You too, sir." Aaron shifts uncomfortably as we take our seats around the dinner table. When Mom brings in the rug rats, we pray and eat together. Aaron and I quickly finish, excuse ourselves, and go to the basement with the flat-screen and game consoles. We started a game of *Mario Kart* for Wii last time he was here, so we just pick up where we left off. I beat him badly twice because he's distracted, texting on his phone. I didn't think he had a girlfriend. I wonder if he's seeing anyone now.

The third time he doesn't finish the race, Aaron tosses the controller away. "You wanna go out and get something to drink?"

"Sure!" I'm grinning from ear to ear, even though we have plenty to drink here. Truth is, I'd love any excuse to go out.

I grab a jacket and trot up the stairs with him in tow. Mom's in the kitchen with Greg, putting up dishes and leftovers. She's in her nursing scrubs, ready for the night shift. Her faded makeup can't hide the bags under her eyes. I know she's tired. She does everything in her power to keep me safe, but surely with Aaron there, she won't say no to something as innocent as a run to the store. I could be doing something much worse, after all.

"Hey, Mom, can we get a Coke from Target?"

Noah yells something, and Abby cries out before Mom answers: "De, I don't think—"

Greg cuts her off. "Honey, it's just a Coke."

My stepdad's cool. And even though I know he's just trying to win points with me, I find it hard to restrain my enthusiasm. Mom hesitates before Noah screams and she almost drops the plates she's holding. "You come straight home, De. Once I'm done here, I'm off to work. So text me when you get back."

"OK," I say with a quick nod as she puts the dishes up and sees to the rug rats. Greg smiles.

"Deidra," Mom calls after me, "remember, Aaron needs to go home at eight!"

"Yeah! Got it!" I want to jump up and down for this small victory but restrain myself as I smile at Aaron and we scoot out the door. I slide into his black Infiniti and buckle up, ready to go. Aaron, however, takes his time and fiddles with his phone again. I don't say anything because I don't want to sound impatient, but I can't understand why he's taking so long.

"Who're you talking to?" I finally ask, afraid my mom will run out of the house at any moment and take back my temporary freedom.

"My parents," Aaron says, and leaves it at that.

"Oh...you need to get back?"

"Not yet," he mumbles.

He seems nervous. I wonder if it has anything to do with me. I want to ask, but all I say is, "Oh," before Aaron finally starts the car. It's a short drive to Target, and the ride is quiet. "Apologize" plays as we park in the back of the almost empty lot and get out. I enjoy the walk, though. The air is refreshing and just a little cool.

Target is eerily quiet as Aaron gets his Coke and I get lemonade. With the skeleton crew, we wait in the checkout aisle awkwardly. I scan through the magazine covers, highlighting articles full of gossip, scandal, and sex tips. Skinny, beautiful girls grace the covers. For the thousandth time, I wish I were more beautiful and didn't have an extra ten pounds to lose.

Sandy-haired Aaron fiddles with his phone, and I wonder if he thinks I'm pretty. His attention skips to anything but me, confirming my fear: I'm not worth looking at.

We've finally checked out and are back in his Infiniti, but Aaron just sits there. Even though I'm already buckled and ready to go, his attention rests on his phone. After a while, I ask: "Why are we waiting so long?"

Aaron's green eyes look up at me, startled, like he forgot I'm here or that we're just sitting doing nothing in an empty parking lot. "Um, I need to hang here." He looks down again. "I'm waiting to get a text back from my parents."

"Oh," I say again. Aaron seems to get even more distant over the next ten minutes as we wait silently in his car. But I start to enjoy the quiet. I let the window down and feel the cool air.

Aaron finally looks up when a white Jeep and burgundy Hummer drive up and stop next to us, playing music. I recognize the girl and guy who step out of the Jeep. They're in my grade at school, but not special ed. Aaron introduced me to them once, and they seem like a lot of fun. Well, more fun than sitting in the parking lot. And a lot more fun than home.

I leave Aaron in the car with his phone.

"Hey. Deidra, right? I'm Jason," he smiles as his black hair falls into his eyes. Wearing a dark shirt and fitted jeans, he's cute in a rocker type of way. I can't help but smile back.

The guy who gets out of the Hummer is short and dark, like maybe he's from India. I realize I've never met him before as the tall, pretty redheaded girl runs up to me. She's in a short skirt and smells like beer. "She *is* cute," she winks. I blush. "I'm Bri, remember? We're off to a party. Wanna come and play pool with us?"

They're the kind of kids who can do whatever they want, when they want. I can't wait the three more months 'til I can, too. Until I can get soft drinks without permission. I look at Aaron, who hasn't moved, not even to greet them. Whatever they're doing has to be more fun than this. "Maybe," I say. "Where at?"

"At a friend's." Jason's voice is smooth and deep. He smirks. His dark eyes and long eyelashes make my stomach flutter before Bri takes my hand and spins me around. "The Way I Are" plays from their car stereo.

"Come on, it'll be fun!" Bri laughs. She dances with me in the empty parking lot, then spins me into Jason's arms before she giggles and lets go. "Your turn, Jason."

I can't find my tongue as I quickly pull away. "Guess I'll owe you a dance at the party, then." Jason smiles, and I manage to nod. I wouldn't mind hanging out with him for a while. After all, we're just going to play pool.

"What do you think, Aaron? Can we go?" I ask my ride, after I run back to his car and lean through the open passenger door.

Aaron hasn't made eye contact with me since we left the store. He finally looks up at the others, then at me. "You wanna go, then go." Aaron fidgets. "I gotta get back."

"No problem, we'll make sure you get home," the other guy assures me with a bright smile and perfect teeth. He's kind of cute, too. "I'm Nikhil, by the way."

"Oh, my bad!" Bri giggles. "Nikhil's going to drive."

"Sounds fun!" I say, then wave bye to Aaron. The rest of us pile into the Hummer. It smells like new leather. "Party Like a Rock Star," "Glamorous," "Crank That," and "Walk It Out" play on our soundtrack as we drive I–65 to Green Hills. Nikhil drums his thumbs against the wheel, and Jason air-guitars in the front while Bri and I dance and sing in the back. It's fun to be with them. I wish I were closer to Jason, though. I like when his dark eyes smile at me.

I'm laughing so much that I can't breathe when Nikhil parks at the mansion that's three times the size of my house. It's all stone and glass windows with a large yard and pond. That's all I notice while Jason leads us to a basement that looks like a club. It's already packed with people, and most of them are older than me. They're drinking and dancing to "SexyBack." I'm about to join them when my phone vibrates.

Mom: "Are you home yet? Did you forget to text me?"

Me: "Yeh sry were just pulling in."

With Mom at work and Greg with the rug rats, I know the lie will buy me some time. I'm grateful for that when Jason smiles and hands me a pool stick. He leans in and whispers, "You're on my team."

When our hands touch, my heart skips a beat. "Don't you want to dance?" I ask.

We watch a few couples grind on each other before Jason says, "Not yet."

Nikhil offers us something to drink. The red liquid smells sweet like punch mixed with alcohol. Jason smiles at me while he takes a drink from his red plastic cup.

I take Nikhil's drink. The music blares as we play against Bri and Nikhil. I'm not any good, though, and within minutes, everything starts to get hazy. The room spins. I don't know if anyone else notices. We keep playing, but my balls never go in the pockets.

"In your face!" Bri jumps around and cheers when her team wins again.

"Yeah, yeah." Jason picks up the pool cues, avoiding me.

I slur, "Next time" as everyone moves to leave. Nikhil gently helps me into the Hummer, and we drive off. The new-leather smell starts to give me a headache.

Mom: "8 pm, De. Has Aaron left yet?"

I have no idea where Aaron is. I barely manage to find the keys to type. Me: "Yeh."

When we drop off Jason and Bri at the Target, Nikhil turns to me and smiles. His white smile is almost blinding. "I'll take you home," he says. "It's on my way anyway."

I get out of the car, hoping Jason will offer to drive me home as well, but he doesn't. Bri smiles and hops into the passenger side of his Jeep. At least I think it's a smile. My head feels kind of clouded. I hug Jason awkwardly and slur, "See ya."

"Yeah, see ya," Jason mumbles, never looking at me. He slides into the Jeep and drives away.

With no other place to go, I climb into the front seat of Nikhil's Hummer. "Thanks," I say as we drive off. My head pounds, and I'm thankful Nikhil doesn't talk. I'm glad I don't have to answer any questions. I'm really tired. My body feels heavy. We're driving for a while before I realize we've passed the exit for my house.

"Where're we going?" I ask, but Nikhil doesn't answer before my phone rings. I groggily pull it out of my pocket, and it slips into the cup holders between us.

"It's OK. I got it." Nikhil grabs my phone, smirks, then powers it off and tosses it out his window. I don't understand what's going on. My head throbs when Nikhil gets off at the next exit. Tears blur my eyes, and my heart starts racing. "Try to get out and I will kill you." His eyes flash angrily as he opens his center console and shows me a gun. I know he means it. His cool temper is gone. He doesn't smile anymore.

We're speeding down Franklin Road, but even so, I try to open the door, but it's no use. I'm child-locked. "Why're you doing this? Where're you taking me?" Soon I'm sobbing so hard I can't breathe.

Nikhil pulls to a stop, aims his gun at me, and yells, "Shut up already!"

We're in the five-car garage at his parents' concrete and stone mansion where he lives, near my school, just minutes from my house. My head spins as Nikhil forcefully pulls me out at gunpoint. I want to scream, but his hand quickly covers my mouth. "Don't even think about it," he seethes into my ear, leaving me in tears, shaking with fear. "You make one sound and I'll kill you and your family. I know where you live."

He pushes the gun against my ribs and shoves me inside. It's late, and although other cars are in the garage, his parents are nowhere to be found. The light inside is dim. I can just make out brightly colored walls, gold accenting, flowing tapestries, and creepy statues I've never seen before. It's all blurry. I want to run, more than anything, but my legs won't work.

His gun pushes me forward.

"You will be quiet," he hisses, locking the bedroom door behind him. He pushes me to the bed, forces me down, and pulls off my clothes. The terror is overwhelming. I mumble and cry, trying to fight, frantically protesting until he stuffs part of my shirt in my mouth. It makes me gag and cough as he pulls my hair and grabs at me hard. He's too strong. Tears sting my eyes.

That's when I'm raped for the first time.

The next morning, I wake up in Nikhil's bed with a splitting headache. My body hurts so much my stomach turns. I feel dirty, but it's the kind of dirt that I know won't wash off no matter how hard I scrub. I try to crawl off the bed, but Nikhil stops me. Naked, I shiver and pull back. He glares before he throws a short skirt and T-shirt at me, then pulls out his gun.

From the bed, I struggle to pull on the clothes while he watches me. He looks disgusted and quickly grows impatient, so I try to hurry. Once I'm fully clothed, he yanks my arm and easily pulls me off the bed. He expects me to stand, but my legs won't hold me up.

Nikhil gives me another red plastic cup, ordering: "Drink it. All of it." I want to cry, but his gun makes me drink every last drop. My head spins again as he shoves me out of the room.

Before I know what's happening, I'm back in his Hummer. This time, he lets me lie down in the back, and I drift in and out of consciousness, never really sleeping. My head aches, and my vision blurs. I realize I have no idea where I am anymore. Nikhil eventually stops at a run-down motel, pulls me out of the car, and forces me into a room. He doesn't stop at the front desk. He already has a key. I wonder if he's been here before. Maybe he planned this.

Inside the room, the door is bolted securely, and Nikhil makes sure I can see his gun. I'm dizzy as he types on his laptop. I want to know what he's doing, and Nikhil notices, sneering, "Go ahead, bitch. You should really see this."

He backs up, allowing me to see a Craigslist ad for a girl named Destiny. She's "A Pretty Blue-Eyed Blond. A sweet young thing looking for a good time.... Need a man to make me moan.... Oral Princess...." There's some other fine print that makes my cheeks blush and a raunchy-looking picture of a girl from behind. Somehow I know Destiny is supposed to be me.

He's going to start pimping me out.

When I start to panic and cry, Nikhil grabs my chin as his lips curl into a sick smile: "Do this and you can go home. Then I won't have to kill your family."

None of this makes any sense. Fear paralyzes me as Nikhil's phone rings and he picks it up. "Yeah. ... Destiny's at the corner of Fourth and Main, room three twenty-two. ... She's worth every penny."

He smirks, closes his phone, then pulls me to the bed and takes off my jacket. I'm freezing and pull away from him, but he yanks me back hard. I fight tears as he forces my eyes to him, whispering angrily, "You will do everything he wants. I'll know if you don't."

Nikhil makes me drink more drugs, packs up, and leaves. I shake uncontrollably. I can't make myself stop. I feel woozy when a man in a suit enters the room. He's as old as my stepdad and light skinned like me. His eyes don't look kind. They look hungry.

"Why don't you dance for me?" the man says as he loosens his tie and takes off his jacket. His stare creeps me out. I'm so frightened I can't think straight, but I remember Nikhil's gun. His threats still ring through my mind.

The man turns on the radio. I don't recognize the song. The noise just hurts my head. I try to move, but I'm too dizzy to stand. The Suit stares me down, so I turn away, trying to hide my tears and dread. My head spins with the room, and I lose my balance in the skinny heels I'm wearing. I steady myself against the wall, wishing to disappear.

"You can do better than that." His voice is right behind me, startling me enough to turn back around. When I do, he's not wearing anything, and he slaps me hard across the face. "You're a naughty slut, aren't you?"

No, I'm not. I don't know what he's talking about. He slaps me again, and I cover my face. Tears sting my eyes, and I crumble onto the bed, pleading: "Stop. Please don't."

But the Suit just keeps moving toward me, lust and hate in his eyes. "You want this."

No, I don't. I don't want any part of this, but for the next hour, the Suit takes all his anger out on me. I'm violated in ways I can't even begin to understand. I try to scream, but he covers my mouth. When he's finally done, he leaves a few bills on the nightstand, dresses, and leaves. I don't remember ever being in so much pain or feeling so ashamed. I want to cry but can't. My voice is gone. My head's swimming.

When I at last muster the strength to pull my clothes on, a younger Hispanic man walks into the room. This guy is more cautious, almost nervous. Maybe he doesn't want to do this anymore than I do.

"Not much time," he says finally. "You help with this?"

The man gestures to his belt, and Nikhil's warnings echo loudly through my mind. I do everything the man wants.

I've not bothered to dress when Nikhil's back. He looks as disgusted as I feel after he collects the money for which I was abused. I can't even remember how many guys came through the door.

I'm tired, but can't sleep. I'm hurting, but so drugged I can't cry. I'm terrified as my body shifts quickly between too hot and too cold. I finally drag myself to the bathroom and see that I'm bleeding now, even though it's not my time of the month. Water and soap won't make me clean. I want to throw up, but there's nothing in my stomach. I want to lock myself in here, away from my kidnapper, away from everything, but Nikhil breaks the lock and drags me out.

"Stupid bitch. You can't hide from me! I own you. Now drink." He forces my mouth open and pours the liquid down. I cough, trying not to choke. My head soon spins again before he commands, "Get dressed. We're leaving."

It takes me a while, but I obey. He still has the gun. He still threatens to kill me if I don't follow his orders.

I don't remember how we got back into his burgundy Hummer. I wonder if this is what it feels like to black out. I watch from the back as Nikhil picks up a guy I've never seen before. He's white and preppy, wearing a dark cap low over his eyes. The new guy hardly acknowledges me. I'm glad he's not another john. "So Biship's letting you in, huh?"

"Yeah, thanks for the hookup. Seems he can't say no to fresh merch," Nikhil says. He laughs, and Preppy rolls joints for them. Somehow I know he's a dealer. They act like old friends.

"No, I'm sure he can't," Preppy says with a laugh. They smoke until the car is filled with the herby smell of pot. I start to cough, and they finally roll down their windows. I try to roll mine down, but it's locked. I wish I could sleep because we drive for a really long time. I stare out the window as the gray interstate turns brown and trees and farmland give way to run-down homes.

Nikhil finally pulls off the interstate in what looks like Memphis. A few skyscrapers hide the older industrial city. We drive in an area where girls are dressed up on the street and guys walk around in gangs. A few people talk together. I think I see them exchange drugs. I'm definitely not in Brentwood anymore. Any hope I had of getting home now is shattered. I did what he asked, but he didn't take me back. Maybe he never means to.

Nikhil finally stops at a beat-up, tan, concrete Motel 6, and we wait in the cracked and faded parking lot. My heart is racing as he speaks into his phone. "We're here."

Two big black guys walk down the outdoor stairs. One is tall and built like a football player. He wears black clothes and a gold chain with a large "B" on it. The other guy is shorter, kind of scrappy. He's in jeans and a red shirt. Nikhil and his friend get out of the Hummer and talk to them. I can't hear anything they say. I don't want to. I just want to wake up from this nightmare.

Finally, Nikhil comes back with a key. "Go to room two thirty-eight. There's food for you there."

His perfect smile doesn't fool me, but when Nikhil shows me his gun again, I do what he says. Room two thirty-eight opens when I knock, and two skinny black girls bring me in. The room is really small and smells musty. The girls have tattoos and piercings and lots of makeup, and a big letter "B" is branded on both their bare shoulders. They don't look much older than me.

"Welcome to da fam'ly," the girl with a pink wig slurs, toasting to me before she sits. "I'm Roxy, an' dat's Coco."

Nausea hits me again as the long-haired girl hands me a plate of food. "You ain't got nuttin' to worry 'bout," she says as she winks. "Daddy's gonna take real good care of you."

She leaves me and smacks Roxy on the head before she takes the drink from her. "Dat's enough, Rox. Biship's not gonna be cleaning up aftah yo' sorry ass again."

Roxy reaches for her drink and whines, "How'd you get tah be bottom bitch anyways? Stupid ho.... "

Coco slaps her and glares. "You'd better start recognizin' yo' place 'round here, Rox.... "

My heartbeat pounds in my ears, drowning out their fight. I try to look at the shrimp and chips in my lap, but I'm not hungry, even though I haven't eaten in almost two days. Their fighting only makes my head hurt worse.

I must've started crying because Coco pulls me into the adjoining room and gives me some pills. "Yo' head hurts, right?" I nod, and Coco shoves the pills into my mouth with some alcohol to swig it down. "Wait here, Destiny. Dey gonna be coming back soon."

She's gentle and kind with me and I wonder if, hope, and pray she'll help me. But as the pills start to take effect, my head hurts worse and the girls go back to arguing. It soon becomes painfully clear: They don't care a thing about me.

I don't know if I dozed off before the two black guys enter the room. They're even bigger and scarier up close. Scrappy hands Coco a plastic shopping bag. It has brightly colored lingerie in it, and he orders us to put it on, but not before Biship grabs me hard by the arm.

"Yo' not gettin dressed yet, Destiny." He pushes everyone out and shuts the door. His breath smells like beer. "Scream, an' I'll kill you."

I believe him. I don't scream. Though I want to cry, I don't. Though I want to fight back, I don't. I know if I do, I'm dead. I'm as good as dead already.

When he's done with me, he yells, "Coco! Fix dis bitch. Damn girl's raggin'. Dere's blood ev'rywhere."

Coco's by my side quickly after that. She tries to drag me to the bathroom, but I can't move, and she's not strong enough to make me. "I just had my period," I mumble into the pillow.

The long-haired girl pulls back and yells to the other guys, "Biship, yo' rufi's* just knockin' her out. She's no good to nobody sleepin'!" Then everything gets really fuzzy, and I black out.

---

* Rufi: A slang term for a powerful sedative drug that is illegal in the United States, commonly known as the "date rape" drug because its ability to cause semi-consciousness and memory blackouts is associated with unwanted sexual encounters.

I doze in and out of sleep before Scrappy's back with kitchen sponges. He gives them to Coco, who takes me to the bathroom. I notice there's blood on the sheets. It's my blood. That's why I hurt so bad.

Scrappy calls the front desk to make up the bed, while Coco helps me put a yellow sponge* up my vagina to stop the bleeding. It hurts even more now. I don't think I can sit down when Coco gives me the lingerie to wear. "It's yo's. Gotta make sure new girl's pretty." She winks, and I realize she's missing a few teeth. I gawk, wondering if someone hit her. I wonder if it was Biship.

"Don' you dare feel sorry fuh me, bitch!" Coco seethes and storms out.

Roxy strolls in with alcohol and drugs. "She in charge of us hoes, so she haftah be like dat." When a cell phone rings, I jump. Roxy smirks. "It's gonna be easier if you enjoy it."

She hands me the cup and pills. I fight back shock and tears. "You enjoy it?"

"Didn' say dat...." she looks down. "I don' have no choice neither. Never had."

"Roxy, I'm in so much pain I can hardly stand," my voice is hoarse and wavers. Roxy ignores me. I start panicking, no longer able to hide my tears. "Can you help me, please? I have to get out! I have to get—"

The knock at the door startles us, and Roxy quickly silences me before Biship yells though the door: "Fix her hair or somethin', too. She got comp'ny in ten."

Roxy sets down the beer and leans toward me, quiet. "Dis life's a bitch. You cain't talk like dat if you wanna live."

Coco's back and must have overheard something because she slaps Roxy hard, then glares at us both. "Quit yo bitchin', both of yas."

---

* Sponge: Instead of being allowed to use tampons, victims are often required to cut up pieces of kitchen sponges and insert them in their vaginas to absorb menstrual blood without the johns noticing, as they would with a tampon.

My heart races. I'm sweating, even though I'm ice cold. Roxy recovers from the slap. She tries to make my hair look full and pretty and darkens my eyes with makeup. When she's finished, I don't recognize myself. The girl in the mirror isn't me.

Scrappy carries his gun into the bathroom. He glares at me, then whispers: "Do what da foo wants. You tell anybody 'bout any of this an' I'll kill ev'ryone who knows you."

I try not to cry as Coco makes me drink more alcohol and drugs. The world gets fuzzy again when they leave my room, but I know they're right there in the adjoining room. They make sure I know that they'll hear if I try to escape.

I wait on the bed all made up, wearing nothing but lingerie. I jump when someone knocks. This time, an older black man walks into the room. He has a beard and mustache. My stomach turns, and I feel short of breath. I hope I pass out.

I wake up to the sound of a cell phone. I realize where I am again and want to cry, but Scrappy is there with me. He gives me more to drink and a bag of chips. A mix of mold, cigarettes, and alcohol hit my nose, and I fight the urge to vomit. My pelvis hurts. The same kitchen sponge is still inside me.

Biship, on the phone, notices my pain. "Do somethin' 'bout dis," he whispers angrily to the girls while he points at me like I'm some kind of animal. Just a body for sale.

After pulling me to the bathroom, Coco tells me to take out the sponge as she fixes my hair and makeup. The sponge hurts with every pull I make; my walls inside are torn and raw. I want to scream but bite through my lip instead. I taste metal when the once-yellow sponge comes out completely red. Blood drips over my hand.

Coco makes me toss it into a plastic bag, then gives me another sponge, expecting me to shove it in. This one's large and green. I know I don't have a choice when Biship opens the door. He looks me over disapprovingly, then tells the girls, "Cover up dem bruises,* too, an' she needs a lil' more color on her face." He turns to me next and says, "Do dis an' you can go home."

I've heard that before, and I don't believe him. His breath smells like beer. He has no intention of ever letting me go, but every intention of hurting me if I don't obey.

"Put da damn sponge in," he orders. "Can't have you grossing out da johns."

I do as he says. He watches as I squirm in pain. I get the sick feeling that he enjoys watching. His phone rings, and I jump. He hands me the lingerie and steps out.

The girls finish, and once again Destiny stares back at me. They leave me alone in the room, waiting again on another john.

More than anything, I want this to end. When the next john's done, he leaves his payment and shuts me in. Everything's so foggy, but not enough to forget my shame or dull any pain. I hurt so much I want to scream, but my mouth won't move. The agony comes out more like a groan.

I think I black out before the pimps come back with food. Biship takes the payment and the food to the other room, while Scrappy leaves the beer and his phone on the table. He catches me staring at him, so he sneers, "Wha' you lookin' at, bitch?"

He comes over fast, threatening to hit me. I cry, and he laughs.

---

* Bruises: Victims are commonly forced to use makeup to cover up bruising on their bodies.

"S'what I dought," he mumbles before he walks into the bathroom and shuts the door.

I don't want to move. I don't feel like I can, but I can't go on like this. I have to do something. While Biship and the girls eat in the other room, I grab Scrappy's phone and hurriedly type the only number that comes to mind. It's Chase's, a boy I liked from last year.

Me: "Feelfunynotle 6 mephgis is De."

I'm woozy and know it's not right, but I barely get the text off when Scrappy's out of the bathroom. He sees the phone and is already glaring. My heart races, especially when the phone beeps in my sweaty hand.

"What the—!" Scrappy yells and throws me onto the bed, furiously grabbing for the phone. He pulls it from me and opens it. Panic fills his dark face, and a string of cuss words fly from his mouth.

Maybe Chase responded.

Biship rushes in and yells at Scrappy. They're both panicking while I slip off the bed and hide behind the chair in the corner of the room. At some point, the phone is thrown to the floor, stomped on, and destroyed. I hope Chase got the message and gets help. I hope he remembers me.

Scrappy paces furiously. The girls fly in, and Roxy whines, "Wha' we gonna do?"

"We needa get outta here," Coco says before Biship slaps her hard across the face.

"Shut up, bitch!"

"She right, D. I ain't dealin' wit' no cops," Scrappy says.

Biship is furious but can't argue. He grabs my clothes and throws them at me. "Put dese on. We goin' tah management." I fumble while dressing, and he yells, "Wha's wrong wit' you, bitch?" before he grabs my arm and shakes me until I fall. He stands over me, fuming, while I recover, grab the clothes, and hastily throw them on. I'm forced out the door with Scrappy leading. Biship holds me tightly and pulls up my hood. He orders, "Keep yo' head down."

I do as he says while we walk down a dirty stairwell and through some old hallways until we reach the main check-in area. Biship holds me back, while Scrappy talks to the guy at the front desk. The clerk's skinny, young, and black. He recognizes Scrappy and quietly takes a payment from him. He knows, and he's in on it. No one's going to help me here.

I want to run, but the room spins, and Biship's grip is strong. My head pounds as I try to listen to Scrappy's hushed words: "Yo, I be needin' a new room."

"I gotcha, Red." The clerk fidgets. "But I wanna see Roxy again."

Scrappy seethes, but nods.

"New floor and everythin'. Comin' right up," the clerk says. He quickly retags keys and hands them to Scrappy. "Room one-twelve. Lemme know if you need anythin' else."

Scrappy takes the keys, and we walk back up the stairwell. Roxy leaves us to move everything to the new room. Just when I lie down again, Biship's cell rings.

"Get 'er ready. An' dis time, try a wig." Biship's orders leave me shaking. They close me in with Coco, preparing me for more johns.

The line of men seems endless. The days mesh into nights, and it starts to sink in that no one is going to help me. The text must not have worked because I'm trapped in the same unending, terrifying routine: Phone rings, I'm made up, they scatter, and I wait for the next guy to walk in and abuse me.

Everything's hazy. I don't see faces anymore. The last guy leaves his money by the door, and when Biship comes in to collect it, he assaults me again. I no longer have the energy or will to cry, much less fight. When he's done, I hide under the blankets.

He turns on the TV and orders porn.

I hear all of it. Everything sounds so sexy, something I never feel when I'm with them. Biship yanks off my covers. "Yo' watchin' dis, bitch. Dis is wat dey want." He sneers at me while an orgy plays out on screen. "You needa learn somethin' if yo' ever gonna make any real bank."

I don't watch, but Biship does until Scrappy runs in with his computer. He's frantic as he shows Biship a screen I can't see.

"Yo, man, check it," he says, and Biship reads, "It's local news, official missin' persons."

Biship swears as his phone rings. I hate that ring. I dread that ring. It signals another john. Biship walks out of the room to arrange details. Scrappy stays and sits in front of the TV while the porn flick plays. He leans back to me. "Dis one's good, Destiny. You do dat," he points to the screen, "an' you won' need Craigslist no more."

I think I'm going to be sick. I stagger to the bathroom, and Coco follows me. Though I'm tainted and nothing can hide that, Coco tries. She gives me more to drink, covers me in makeup, and stuffs my hair under a short blond wig. Too soon, Destiny stares back at me.

I've lost track of time. Days and hours feel like years in this hell. I thought I knew what prison felt like, but I was wrong. I'd give anything to be home now.

My mind's cloudy when the pimps leave me alone to wait on the next john. The room is as empty as I feel. The adjoining door is open, but no one peers in on me from the other side. The girls are both there, though. They're still loud.

Soon my head starts to pound. It sounds like metal hammering against wood, like the wood's going to break. That's when I see the hotel room door cracking. It's not my head, but the door that's pounding open when a voice booms: "This is the FBI! Step away from the door!"

The next blow is even louder. The girls are quiet now. Coco runs in and drags me into their room, locking all the doors. We're hiding, shocked, and silent, but the banging doesn't stop.

I feel like I'm in a daze. Part of me wants to run and open the door, but I can't tell if I'm dreaming or awake, so I just watch while the other girls hold me still.

"Stand back! Stand back!" the cops shout before they kick in the door and storm into the room I was just in. Police lights start flashing outside. They bang on our door now, and in a matter of moments, it's kicked down, too. Cops rush in. "FBI. Freeze! Show me your hands! Hands up! On the ground! On the ground!"

I'm frozen, but the girls try to run. The cops quickly grab them, though. "Get yo' hands off me!" Coco yells.

"Ma'am! Calm down," a lady cop yells. "Sit down or we'll make you." Even when the girls fight back, the cops have them handcuffed fast. Coco and Roxy are too skinny to put up much of a fight anyway.

I haven't moved since we started hiding, and when the other girls are secure, a lady cop helps me into the other room. A guy cop comes with her and watches while she sits me on the bed. "Everything's going to be OK," she says. "We're going to take you home now." The lady cop then moves to address the other girls, who still won't shut up.

"Stop touchin' me! Biship don' want no cops touchin' me. He's gonna be g'ttin' back soon, an' he'll be pissed!" Coco yells. I just sit there watching.

"Where is your pimp?" the lady cop yells at them. "Where is he?"

Roxy whines. "I didn' hurt nobody. Please, don' take me!"

"Where is Biship?" the cop yells again. The girls keep talking, but they don't answer any of the cops' questions. I'm too tired and dazed to speak, even if I knew the answers.

Eventually, the FBI agents lead us out of the Motel 6, and when I'm outside, I realize it's nighttime. Everything's foggy, but I dare to hope I'm not dreaming, that this nightmare might finally be ending. That I might finally be going home.

Roxy and Coco are pushed into the back of patrol cars while I'm in the back of an FBI SUV. The lady cop and a guy cop sit in the front. The lady gives me something to eat. It's fast food, but I'm starving. Safe inside the car, I eat it all before my eyelids grow heavy. It's a long ride, and the FBI agents are nice enough to let me sleep.

Three hours later, we arrive home. I don't really believe it. Truth is, I'm afraid to. I don't want to wake up and not be here. My family comes out of the house as we drive up. The cops help me out, and my eyes meet the ground, but not before I see the tears in my mom's eyes. The night air chills me as the rug rats hug me first. "We missed you so much," Noah cries.

My mom hugs me next, and I finally relax in her arms, embracing the hope that this is real. Her hold is strong, and tears of my own fall before she finally calms enough to speak. "I've never been so scared. You're home now, De. I love you, and I'm so sorry." My face is buried in her short blond hair, my eyes blurry with tears. "I'm so sorry I couldn't protect you."

I have no words, no more energy, so I just cry until my knees finally give. I'm so exhausted and broken that my mom can't keep me from falling, so Greg gently helps hold me up. I hear Mom whimpering beside me as my hair is brushed off my face. My family huddles around me, trying in vain to protect me from the world.

The cops still haven't left yet. They've been silent until now, letting us reunite. When the lady cop approaches, my mom wipes her eyes and mumbles earnestly, "Thank you."

"It's an honor, ma'am. But before we pack up, I have to inform you that Deidra needs a sexual assault exam. She's carrying evidence, so she can't shower or clean up until after that." I shudder inside my mom's arms while she continues. "Memorial Hospital is set up for it. With what she's been through, I'd let her rest before taking her in. We'll have a police escort meet you there and a call-ahead for you in the morning."

When Mom nods, the cops leave us. Greg and Mom help me inside and tuck me into bed. I'm not allowed to change clothes. Mom stays with me through the night, and I know now that I'm home.

Mom lets me sleep a little, but the pain I feel is unbearable. The sponges are still inside me, and the phone keeps ringing, startling me into panic with each new call, reminding me of the Memphis motel room. My mom finally helps me get ready, and we drive to the ER. I've never been in so much pain or felt so gross.

It is 8:00 a.m. There's no police escort, no call-ahead, so we stand in a triage line that doesn't move. I feel like everyone can see where I've been and what I've done. I wear my shame like the small tank top and shorts I'm still in. Exhaustion wears on me, but the sponges keep me alert, sending shooting pain through my stomach and down my legs every time I move.

Three security guards near us complain to each other, "My back's out again. I can't keep standing all day like this."

"That's what I keep telling management! Let us use some chairs every once in a while, right?" a butch woman argues, but eventually I stop listening. They never look up or notice us. My missing-person poster is on the wall beside them.

Mom and I keep waiting as the line slowly creeps forward. By now I can hardly stand. My mom finally pulls out her phone and dials my special ed counselor. When Ms. Cindy picks up, I hear my mom whisper, "Do we have to come here?"

The guard finally notices her. "Ma'am, you can't talk on the phone there."

"Excuse me?" my mom almost yells.

"You can't talk on your phone there, Ma'am. You must be over there," she points to a spot five feet away. I watch as my mom clenches her fists and takes the two steps away from me to talk on the phone. Drowsiness kicks in, but I hear phrases from my mom's conversation.

"This is ridiculous. ... Is there no other place we can have her examined?" My mother wrings her hands through her hair. She sighs and at last mutters "thanks" before she hangs up.

Eventually, the triage nurse calls us back. She's next to my poster but never bothers to look at us. She doesn't even ask for identification.

"What're you here for?" she asks her clipboard.

"She's been a victim of sexual assault, and we have to have an exam," my mom says, trying to steady her wavering voice. Minutes seem to tick by, and Mom's losing her cool.

The nurse finally looks up, around the room. "Well, where are the police? Did you bring the police?"

I don't know where they are, and neither does my mom. She's furious, especially when the butch security guard steps closer to listen in outside the door. "I'm going to close the door. I think we need a little privacy," Mom tells the nurse, then slams the door in the guard's face.

"Ma'am, there's nothing I can do for you. There's been no call-ahead, and I can't do anything until the police get here," the nurse says again.

"She's in pain. ... She's got these sponges," Mom pleads. "Where am I supposed to go?"

I'm drowsy and can't look at her. I can't speak. Finally, the nurse sighs and says, "Would it make you feel better if I called the rape support advocate?"

"What's the rape support advocate gonna do?" Mom's eyes are wet as she yells, "Yes, please call all those freaking people, but she needs to see a doctor now!"

The nurse remains cold. She still hasn't asked our names or if we are related.

Fifteen minutes later, my pelvis hurts so bad that I keel over and groan from the shooting pain. Mom finally loses it. She slams her hand hard against my missing-person poster, yelling, "Do you see that picture right there? That's her."

"Oh, OK," is all the nurse says.

"OK? My daughter's been missing for eight days!"

The woman finally, reluctantly, stands up and brings us farther into the hospital. She puts me on a gurney in the hallway and leaves us there. She never comes back.

We wait there for hours. I want to fall asleep, but it's so cold. The pain in my pelvis is getting worse.

"What's going on?" Mom asks anyone who passes by. "We've been waiting here forever." No one responds. "My daughter's been missing. ... She needs a sexual assault exam."

She pleads through tears, and I try to drown out her words. I don't want to hear them. I don't want to hear anything.

Finally, the officer stationed there comes over to my mom. "I know who she is and what you've been through. I want you to know that I'm going to take care of this."

My mom quietly utters thank you as the cop leaves us in the hallway. Not long after that, a man with glasses and a clipboard wearing a long, white coat comes up and tries to talk to me. "So you've been sexually assaulted? Where have you been sexually assaulted?"

I'm sleepy, and his eyes are too intense. "What?" I mumble out. "I don't know what you're talking about. Where?"

With little patience, the doctor repeats, "They sexually assaulted you. Where did they stick their penis? In your mouth? Vagina? Anus?"

"What?" I mumble, confused and horrified because I don't want to admit to any of it, especially not in a crowded hallway. But the man just repeats the question louder. Now the whole section of the hospital can hear him. I can't help but cry.

"Stop! Just stop!" my mom yells, and he quiets. "Who the hell do you think you are?"

The man collects himself. "I'm Dr. Dennis Hughes, and I'm a physician's assistant. I'm the head of the sexual exam unit."

"I'm not doing this in the hallway," my mom fumes.

"We will have to wait for a room to open up, then. As soon as the one across the way is open, we'll take you in," he says, then leaves us.

Half an hour later, a guy in handcuffs is rolled out, and I'm rolled in. The room is freezing. The thermometer reads 65 degrees. No one bothers to turn up the heat or give me a blanket. We wait two more hours, and no one checks on us.

Finally, Dr. Hughes comes back in, ready to escort us to the exam room. It's in the very back of the building. The doctor's calm—nice, even—but only when the rape support advocate arrives. She's dark-skinned with long hair, like Coco from Motel 6. They ask how I'm doing, but tears fill my eyes, and my heart races when they make my mom leave. With the doctor and the black woman there, I feel like I'm back in the Memphis motel room.

They pull out the sponge, and I choke back a scream. I nearly pass out from the pain, but the exam keeps me frightened and alert. Their gloved hands and cold utensils probe me, doing things I don't want them to do, reminding me of things I don't want to remember. They silently go through every scratch, bruise, tear, hair, everything. Without my mom present, no one bothers to sympathize or care. I'm not treated as a person; I'm treated as evidence.

Without any breaks, three hours later, we're done. It's 4:00 p.m., and I'm just glad to go home. We don't talk on the ride back. I don't want to. I just want to rest and forget.

But I can't. We pass Nikhil's house, and his threats ring loud in my ears: "You make one sound, and I'll kill you and your family…. I know where you live." I cover my ears and cry.

"Deidra, what's wrong?" my mom asks. I see Nikhil's face in my mind. I feel his gun against my side. I cannot force my mouth open. My mom pulls over the car, desperate: "De. Sweetheart?" she softly pulls my hands from my ears and finds my eyes. "What's wrong?"

Her tears break me. I look away and point to the mansion behind us. "That's where he lives," my voice cracks. "Mom, he knows where we live, and he has a gun, and…."

The words fall out of my mouth. Once I start, I can't stop. My mom cries, and in that moment I see her, I realize that nothing is ever going to be the same again.

We change everything we do from that day on. When we arrive home, she starts adding to the home security. Really high-tech stuff. A police officer even stops by the next day and says he'll keep an eye on us.

My parents make me stay with a friend outside of town. Leiper's Fork is beautiful and calm. The Andersons have horses and lots of land and don't live less than five minutes from my kidnapper's house. I'm glad to be able to relax, to not panic every time I hear the phone ring.

A few days later, I have to go back to Nashville to give the details of my experiences. I'm still foggy from the drugs while three FBI agents wait on my testimony. I'm thankful one of the cops is a lady. They have a camera on me. My palms sweat. I'm so nervous that my throat closes up, and I have to drink lots of water. The cops are not allowed to prompt me. They'll ask questions if they have to, but it's up to me to remember and say everything.

I don't want to talk about it, though. I don't want to remember. When they see how much I struggle, the lady cop whispers, "Have Rodriguez call in the child forensic psychologist."

"OK, Deidra," says a guy cop. "Is it all right if I ask you some questions?" I manage to look up and nod. "All right, tell us what happened when Aaron took you to the store."

We start from the beginning. They ask about the kidnapping, the drinks that made my head spin, the assaults, the Craigslist profile, the pimps and johns. They want all the details. It's hard. The questions help a lot, but I still struggle to talk. I can't remember everything.

"That's fine, Deidra. You did great," the lady cop affirms before she lays out a bunch of photos. "Now, can you identify the men who held you? Are their pictures here?"

My throat tightens when I see their faces. Scrappy, Biship, and Nikhil are all there. Their cold eyes stare back at me, threatening me even when they're not here.

"Deidra?" she asks again, concern in her voice. "Are the men who held you in these photos?" I feel like they are in the room with me now, and terror paralyzes me.

I breathe in deep, fighting tears, but I point them out.

The lady cop smiles and says, "Thank you. That will be all for today."

I may not be able to give the cops enough detail about what happened to me, but I can point out faces. At least I'm able to do that.

A few days later, I go back and meet the child forensic psychologist. Dr. Carolynn's nice. She takes me to a new room with softer chairs and brighter colors. She lets me draw while we talk.

When we're done, she tells my mom, "That was a piece of cake! Got everything we needed, and she's no worse for the wear."

The truth is, I feel more worn than any seventeen-year-old ever should.

The cops assure my mom that they have enough to arrest Nikhil now. "With the progress she's made, she'll be able to withstand cross-examinations by his top attorneys."

"Will she have to go to trial?" my mom whispers. "I don't want her to have to see that monster."

"Ma'am, I assure you, your daughter won't have to look at that son of a bitch ever again." For that I am thankful.

With just a few months until graduation, I can't go back to class. It's not that I don't want to. I really want to see my friends again, but it's not safe, and enough people say I'm not ready. I finally agree to homeschooling, and at the end of the school year, I walk the stage with my classmates and get my diploma.

After graduation, the Andersons drive me back home. We're stopped at a light in Brentwood when Nikhil stops next to us in a gold Buick. Biship and Scrappy are with him. My heart races as I try to hide. Tears reach my eyes, and Mrs. Anderson asks, "Deidra, what's wrong?"

"That's him," is all I can say.

"Well, you lean your seat right back, now," she says before calling to report their license plate number. I lean the seat back and cry.

In the daytime, I hide at the Andersons' home, riding horses, trying to forget. But at night, there's nowhere to hide. Biship, Scrappy, and Nikhil haunt my sleep. Their threats plague my nightmares. My phone rings, and I barely hear it. It's my mom this time. I can't speak, so I let it go to voicemail. She sends a text moments later.

Mom: "Good news!! Check your VM. I love you. ☺"

I listen to the message: "Hey, De. I love you, sweetheart. I wanted you to know that the FBI picked Nikhil up pimping and pandering in Memphis. It seems the cops had trouble getting witnesses together against him and the other pimps.... They made a lot of threats."

I break out in a cold sweat. I know they will make good on them. I fear for my life and my family again, wondering for the hundredth time if I did the right thing, if this trial is going to help anything.

My mom continues, "But Jason and Bri are giving their statements today. Sounds like they were both in Nikhil's gang. He was working to start his own prostitution ring. I'm sorry, honey. They admit to selling you out for drugs."

My stomach turns. I just barely make it to the toilet before I vomit.

"And the cops talked to Aaron, too." I bring the phone back to my ear. Aaron, who took me to the Target parking lot, fiddled with his phone, and waited for texts. That Aaron. "Honey, he never admitted to anything."

Nikhil's parents try to get him out on bail. They have the money to do it, too. His parents turn out to be the heads of trade to Southeast Asia for the State of Tennessee, so they're extremely connected, politically. All my parents' friends know who they are. I would have, too, if I ever read the paper. Today, for instance, Nikhil's dad's business trip to India is one of the headlines.

Everyone at home is freaking out. They're afraid Nikhil's going to leave the country. Terror rises in me again. If he gets out, he will kill me. He will kill everyone I love, and then he'll be gone forever.

Graciously, the judge denies Nikhil's release. Something about having no accountability and supervision by being employed by his dad. A dad who everyone knows—because of his job and highly publicized business trips—is never around. If anyone else held Nikhil accountable, they would have let him out. I'm thankful for this small miracle.

Nikhil's parents spare no expense at the trial, though. They patiently watch every proceeding and support their son, the gangbanging, drug-dealing rapist. They try to portray my kidnapper as a stand out guy and me as a crazy, lovesick girl. They review all of my records. Every therapist, every school, psychologists—everything. They say it was really my fault. "Nikhil did nothing wrong. It was all consensual."

Like I would agree to be pimped out to random strangers, old men, fat men, all hurting me until I'm scared and bleeding, taking their pleasure at the price of my youth and innocence.

The attorneys argue nonstop about why I'm not there. "Who is this victim, anyway?"

I'm so glad I don't have to go. That I don't have to see him again. That my mom found a victim's rights attorney from the Voice of Victims. It's free, too. At the trial, she sits beside the US Assistant Attorney to give presence to my absence. We even have a social worker who works with them.

On September 11, 2009, Nikhil is sentenced to prison. He pleads guilty to all counts. Biship and Scrappy are still free, though. My attorney tells us the cops wanted Nikhil to flip on the other pimps, but he didn't because he knew they would kill him.

The Fray's "You Found Me" and Beyonce's "Halo" play on the radio when we drive home in the SRX. This time, I don't mind Noah and Abby's screaming or my mom's overprotection. I'm looking forward to moving again, to starting over. I like moving. I just feel like you get a fresh start. You don't know anybody. Nobody knows anything about you.

Even with my kidnapper behind bars, I know my life will never be the same again. But that won't stop me from living it.

A MOM'S VOICE

Intervention

As soon as we knew Deidra was not where she was supposed to be, we sounded the alarm. I begged and pleaded for help, and thankfully, we lived in a community that was willing to support us. They became a part of everything we were going through. Anything people could or were willing to do, we would let them. This included putting up missing-person posters and pressing back on law enforcement when they said that Deidra had run away and there was nothing they could do.

The first thing I did was send out an e-mail to my contacts, asking for help. Then I went through Deidra's room, searching through every nook and cranny. I examined everything, even if it was just a little scribble on a piece of paper that had been wadded up. Then I called people, including all of Deidra's friends and contacts. I also knocked on doors, even if it was at 10:00 or 11:00 at night, and spoke with the local paper and news stations. And, in case the police were right, I also searched various places to which Deidra might have run away.

Even with all the searching, days passed and we heard nothing. Deidra's friend never reported the text she sent to him. My urgency and panic grew exponentially. I knew something was wrong. I was actively looking, calling law enforcement multiple times a day, asking if they had heard anything at all about my daughter, but we still had no leads. Though local law enforcement was doing everything they could do, they were not experts. The experts were the Innocence Lost Task Force, a division of the FBI. They were the ones who found my daughter.

I never would have reached them if not for a mother in our community. She had the connections, went to the head of the FBI task force and said, "You need to investigate this, and you need to do it now. I know this family, and I'm telling you right now, their daughter is missing, and something is wrong. Can you please just look at the information? That's all I'm asking you to do—look at the information."

The FBI task force found my daughter within five hours. That is unheard of. Statistically, after seventy-two hours, it is almost impossible to find a kidnapping victim. After a week, the odds of finding a victim are less than 0.1 percent, because by that time, they could have been transported anywhere in the world. Deidra was missing for eight days, yet we found her.

Fortunately, we beat the odds because we had people who were so passionate about seeing justice prevail and willing to help in any way they could. That mother in our community was willing to storm the FBI and validate our story. It is nothing short of a miracle that my daughter was rescued.

Healing

Restoration is not a destination, it's a journey. Every day has its own challenges and victories. It is a conscious choice to get up in the morning, go forward, and do something positive.

Deidra is on her own journey and continues to walk in a positive direction, and for that I am very, very thankful. It has been helpful that, as I have become involved in different groups within the anti-trafficking movement, Deidra has been surrounded by people who love on her. It has been amazing and extremely cathartic having that community around her.

Even with that support, day-to-day life can be a struggle, and that is important for people to understand. Her mental developmental deficits protected and insulated her from some of the extent of this evil, but she still has bad days. The trauma affects Deidra to the point where sometimes she is physically ill. Some nights, she wakes up in complete terror from nightmares and flashbacks.

This is not like a physical wound where you get cut—it hurts and bleeds, but then the bleeding stops, the body starts to restore itself and it eventually heals. Sometimes you never even know the wound was there. This is a deep, emotional wound, and there may be things that Deidra deals with forever.

It is important to remember that survivors need time and strong support systems through this process. Our job as family and friends is to patiently and lovingly walk alongside them on this journey to restoration.

My daughter is an amazing young lady, resilient and able to bounce back. The recovery she has made through this trauma has been astounding. It has been a blessing to see the healing and restoration in our own lives and to be a part of it in so many other lives as well.

My daughter, Deidra, was rescued. After fearing that she was lost forever, I cannot even begin to put into words the joy, relief, and thankfulness we feel to have our daughter back.

Despite the relief of her rescue, we often felt exploited, raw, and alone. This crime of child sex trafficking is so evil and so perverse. It is unlike anything I have ever been exposed to. Once this kind of trauma and abuse has been introduced into a family, it is devastating. It felt like we lost everything.

Every member of my immediate family needed to receive counseling to deal with the profound pain, torment, and fear we experienced. There are still pimps out there who have never been caught or prosecuted, and they know who we are and where we live. Their original threats to kill us still haunt our thoughts. While we are well aware of this present danger, we still have to be able to live our lives. Through many hours of therapy, I finally got to a point where I decided I will be damned if I let the criminals take more from me than they have already taken. I am thankful that I can now say and walk that out with conviction.

The turning point for me was when I delivered the victim impact statement for my daughter at her perpetrator's trail. In front of the court, I read what I would say to the kidnapper. I didn't think I would be able to do it. The fear was overwhelming. After it was over, I found out that there were people in the court—from the probation system, FBI, and police force— who left that room in tears. It was surprising to hear that what I had to say was so impactful.

From that point on, I decided not to be silent anymore. I can be a voice for these girls and tell anyone who will listen that this is happening here— everywhere—and we need to do something about it. I will go anywhere and speak to anyone about this crime—government institutions, school districts, ministries, and filmmakers. My daughter was even able to tell her story on a national television show last year.

A few women in my community wanted to help as well, so we partnered with a local anti-sex-trafficking organization for a fund-raising run. Together, we have been able to raise more than one hundred thousand dollars for organizations that help girls who have been trafficked.

Also, I recently completed forensic-exam training so that, as a nurse, I can be a sexual assault examiner. By obtaining my bachelor of science in nursing with a focus on public health, I am able to branch out into combating the crime of sex trafficking and raise awareness for this vulnerable generation of at-risk children and teens. Though our experiences with

Deidra were damaging and painful, I have been able to use what we learned to change lives.

The unfortunate truth is that this is real. It happened to my daughter. Right now, my daughter can come home and sleep safely in her bed, and I can love on her. But there are thousands of daughters who have been deprived of that safety and love, and that will never be OK with me. My fight will never be over until those daughters are safe. I have chosen to give my life so that others are empowered, encouraged, and compelled to fight this crime of child sex trafficking.

Words To the Wise

Because of Deidra's cognitive and developmental delays, I was a very protective mom. She did not hang out with people we did not know. I knew her friends, met their parents, and supervised her Internet access. I did everything I could to protect her. But the bottom line is, when Deidra was in that parking lot, approached by a perpetrator and given alcohol laced with drugs, there was nothing else I could have done.

The key to Deidra's discovery was that I knew where she was, whom she was with, and when she was supposed to be home. When she did not come home in time, I was able to act immediately.

When I speak to kids, I try to tell them that there should be someone in their lives who always knows where they are and whom they are with. It is so important to keep parents or a trusted adult in the inner circle. For us, that meant the difference between my daughter's life being saved and her falling off the face of the earth.

Part III

SO YOU WANT TO MAKE A DIFFERENCE

Everyone must do his or her part—no one person or agency can end child trafficking alone.

Chapter 8

YOU DON'T HAVE TO BE A ROCK STAR: EVERYDAY PEOPLE MAKING A DIFFERENCE

Now that you have read these true stories and heard from the survivors themselves, how are you feeling? Are you shocked it's happening here in our democratic, first-world country? Are you outraged by the viciousness of the crimes? Likely both. My hope is that you are in some way "marked" by the startling reality of what American children are facing—not just occasionally, but *regularly*. It is time to step up and take responsibility for what we know to be true. Our children deserve every freedom outlined in our great national document the Declaration of Independence, especially the rights of *life, liberty, and the pursuit of happiness.*

The adage, "it takes a village" rings true when fighting a horrific crime such as child sex trafficking. This issue can seem so dark— and frankly, just too overwhelming—to even tackle. Yes, it is dark, and yes, it can be overwhelming, but it's just like any other problem that needs to be tackled one step at a time. There's no one person, one agency, or even one point of view that can bring this to an end. It takes everyone doing the one thing he or she can do, and eventually each of those things adds up to some form of actual change. Ultimately, lives are saved.

Probably the most frequent question people ask me is, "What can I do to make a difference?" My response also is a question, "Well, what are you passionate about? Let that lead you into what you can do." Rest reassured, you don't have to quit your job and start a nonprofit, move to the projects, or adopt a high-risk youth to make a difference. Of course, do all of these if you are truly compelled, but for most of us, those aren't viable options. So what are some options?

Many people are using their passion and expertise to combat child trafficking in their own spheres of influence. I've included some of their following stories to motivate and encourage you.

JOSH M., FOUNDER
McAfee Institute

"When we started, we were focused mostly on fraud detection and loss prevention in the e-commerce world. But in 2010, when we launched our social media investigation course, we had our first human trafficking case. In that class, we teach people from law enforcement agencies and the fraud and loss prevention units of businesses how to find bad guys on Facebook and Twitter, then use the information to prosecute. We never intended to go after human trafficking, but we started seeing more and more cases coming through…. Since 2011, our company has helped bring back about 1,900 human trafficking victims, 1,000 of them kids…. To be able to do this kind of work in my business is everything to me."[1]

ALEXIS L., COFOUNDER
GS GEMS: Girl Scouts

"I was just fourteen when four of my fellow Girl Scouts and I formed GS GEMS, Girl Scouts Empowering and Mentoring with Support. The idea came when my mom showed me an invitation to a Girl Scout event about child trafficking. After attending and learning about the horrors girls were going through, I just knew we had to do something about it. We formed our Girl Scout group with a focus on raising awareness and raising funds to end sex trafficking by making black-and-white awareness jewelry, and by giving presentations using a website I created, www.teensontrafficking.org. Through the years, our commitment to fight trafficking is still strong. As a second-year student at Arizona State University, I remain committed to the GS GEMS and serve as co-leader of the troop. What we began back in 2008 is still growing, with the next generation of young leaders taking up the mission to stamp out child sex trafficking. Founding the GS GEMS has had a huge impact on my life. It helps the greater good and helps me know about myself, the kind of leader I am. Even though there are really awful things in the world, you don't have to sit idly by. You can put your foot down and say, 'This has to be stopped!' I want to encourage other youth that you're never too young to make a difference."[2]

DINA H.
Licensed Specialist in School Psychology

"In 2011, I took a training class on domestic minor sex trafficking (DMST), thinking that I wanted to be educated should I possibly have contact with a victim. The very next day, I had a student in my office whose story was riddled with the 'red flags' I was taught in the previous day's training. I immediately contacted the trainer and discussed the red flags. We then contacted law enforcement, and it was confirmed that the child was being trafficked. From that day forward, I was determined to get the word out and educate our staff. I have since partnered with our school leadership in developing and teaching a curriculum to identify, respond to, and report child sex trafficking for our school district."[3]

CHELSEA D.
Mom

"She's not rich. Chelsea is just a regular stay-at-home mom (who had two little ones younger than two) who felt the call of God in her life—the desire to help these helpless, victimized children and set them free. She's got a loving mother's heart. She decided that she could do something about the situation and started a jewelry business (Justice Juels), which donated a majority of its profits to organizations that rescue children and prosecute criminals for this heinous crime."[4]

KELLY M.
Founder, Dining for Dignity

"Last Friday, I discovered that Chinese companies were selling sex dolls in the image of very young girls to a worldwide customer base. Complete with sexually graphic descriptions and pedophile reviews, the dolls were created to fulfill the lust of those seeking young children for sex. Realizing the power of Facebook and Twitter, I created a social-media blast calling for the immediate removal of these dolls. Dedicated to the cause, hundreds worldwide joined the social media blitz, tagging '@dhgate' on each post. Sunday morning, DH Gate removed the products and committed to its stance against promoting pedophilia. *Huffington Post UK* covered our cause in the Sunday morning edition, and that set off an unstoppable wave of international attention. Within two days, our concerted efforts achieved our goal and caught the world's attention. Our campaign page was being sent to thousands! Our Facebook page received four hundred new followers within a couple of days, and my phone buzzed nonstop with activity!

"For the next few days, we kept the pressure on other Chinese companies—Alibaba.com and Ali Express—because the same products and more were being sold through their sites. Once they became aware, they pulled the dolls and issued a strong stance against the selling of pedophilia products on their sites. A rep from Hong Kong called and e-mailed to follow up."[5]

SOPHIA G.
Child Abuse Pediatrician

"As a child abuse pediatrician, I see so many kids who are unloved, ignored, abused, and highly susceptible to child sex trafficking. For years, I was unaware of the issue, not knowing the signs to look for. Today, I do. After seeing a DMST flier at church then hearing a radio broadcast, my eyes were opened. Now I'm on a mission to educate health-care professionals and the public about the issue. Together with the media relations department at my hospital, we've created a bilingual awareness flier. This flier is sent home with parents of children who receive wellness checks through neighborhood clinics located in high-risk communities. We are beginning to make a difference in our community. My commitment in the fight against child trafficking is easy to pursue because I'm passionate about it."[6]

Each of these people were determined to make a difference from where they were. They considered their circumstances, decided what they could do practically, and took action. Now, it's your turn. If you are passionate about ending child sex trafficking in America, then it's time to blog, tweet, tell a neighbor, start a group, fund an organization—*just do something.*

> *"The only thing necessary for the triumph of evil is for good men to do nothing."*
>
> —Edmund Burke

Knowing what to look for and how to respond could save the life of a child.

Chapter 9

IDENTIFYING AND REPORTING A POTENTIAL VICTIM

AFTER READING THE OVERVIEWS and stories, I imagine your brain and emotions are on high alert to detect potential victims. This information can be very effective when used wisely—and equally dangerous when used emotionally and irresponsibly. With that in mind, I think it's important to give you basic tools to identify, respond to, and report an incident accurately and safely. Note: Typically, no one indicator is enough to identify a victim—multiple indicators should be present.

Red Flags To Watch for:

- Truancy
- Clothing that is inappropriate for the weather or other conditions
- A demeanor that is either withdrawn, depressed, and fearful, or one that is confident and boasting
- The presence of an older, controlling boyfriend or female companion

- Not being allowed to talk
- Being handled roughly or touched inappropriately
- Malnourished or eats as if ravenously hungry
- Sudden change in attire, behavior, possessions
- Branding, tattoos, or carvings
- Evidence of mutilation
- Scripted answers, inconsistent stories
- Frequent travel to other cities
- Varied stages of bruising, with clumps of makeup covering marks
- Possession of motel room cards, escort service cards, condoms, large amounts of cash, or gift cards
- Lack of proper documents (school identification, driver's license, Social Security card)
- Use of terms common to the sex industry
- Stunted growth
- Poorly formed or rotted teeth

I would like to extend a sincere thank you to Deena Graves, founder of Traffick911, for providing me with a significant portion of these red flags.

How to respond if you are a member of the public:

- Call 911 if you believe a child is in immediate danger.
- Contact local law enforcement and give a description of the indicators just listed that lead you to believe the child is a trafficking victim.
- Traffickers are extremely dangerous criminals. *Never* approach a trafficker. Do not attempt to talk to a victim when she is

under the direct supervision of a trafficker. Victims will be moved quickly if the trafficker suspects that he or she has been identified and will often suffer severe beatings for talking with people other than prospective clients.

- Always follow up your experience with a call to the National Human Trafficking Center for data collection purposes.

National Human Trafficking
Resource Center (NHTRC)
1-888-3737-888
www.TraffickingResourceCenter.org

Hotline call specialists are available twenty-four hours a day to take reports from anywhere in the country related to potential trafficking victims, suspicious behavior, and locations where trafficking is suspected to occur. All reports are confidential. Interpreters are available.

How to respond if you are a child advocacy professional:

If you are a professional who could come into contact with survivors of commercial sexual exploitation, I recommend that you take a look at these excellent resources:

- "Sex Trafficking: Identifying Cases and Victims," National Institute of Justice, http://nij.gov/journals/262/Pages/sex-trafficking.aspx

- "Tools for Service Providers and Law Enforcement," Polaris Project, http://www.polarisproject.org/resources/tools-for-service-providers-and-law-enforcement

Resources to equip you for success.

Chapter 10

LEARN MORE: AGENCIES AND RESOURCES

AGENCIES AND INITIATIVES

Now that human trafficking is a hot issue, many new organizations are forming, and I cannot list them all. I have chosen to list in alphabetical order the nationally recognized NGOs and government agencies whose majority of work is to eradicate child sex trafficking in the United States.

Abolition International
www.abolitioninternational.org

Abolition International provides after-care homes and working groups around the world with resources that ensure quality care for survivors of human trafficking.

Courage Worldwide
www.courageworldwide.org

This organization builds homes around the world for children rescued from sex trafficking.

Demand Abolition
www.demandabolition.org

Demand Abolition is committed to eradicating the illegal commercial sex industry in the United States—and, by extension, the world—by combating the demand for purchased sex.

ECPAT–USA
www.ecpatusa.org

This is the leading policy organization fighting Commercial Sexual Exploitation of Children (CSEC) by raising awareness of the issue; advocating for the victims; developing policy for private companies, law enforcement, and government bodies to fight the problem; and passing legislation that protects victims, and penalizes traffickers and exploiters.

Exodus Cry
www.exoduscry.com

Exodus Cry is built on a foundation of prayer and committed to abolishing sex slavery through Christ-centered prevention, intervention, and holistic restoration of trafficking victims.

FAIR Girls
www.fairgirls.org

FAIR Girls prevents the exploitation of girls worldwide with empowerment and education.

GEMS
www.gems-girls.org

Girls Educational & Mentoring Services (GEMS) is the only organization in New York state specifically designed to serve girls and young women who have experienced commercial sexual exploitation and domestic trafficking.

The Grace Network
www.thegracenetwork.org

This organization's mission is to mobilize, train, and assimilate passionate people into all spheres of the anti-trafficking fight, and to identify, share, and celebrate viable resources that meet the specific needs of exploited youth.

Innocence Lost, Federal Bureau of Investigation
www.fbi.gov/about-us/investigate/vc_majorthefts/cac/innocencelost

The FBI, the Department of Justice's Child Exploitation and Obscenity Section, and the National Center for Missing & Exploited Children address the domestic sex trafficking of children in the United States. The organizations developed sixty-six dedicated task forces and working groups throughout the United States, combining efforts of federal, state, and local law enforcement agencies and US Attorneys offices.

Innocents at Risk
www.innocentsatrisk.org

The mission of this organization is to educate citizens about the grave issue of global and local human trafficking. It is dedicated to protecting children from all forms of abuse, and is working to end child exploitation and child trafficking everywhere.

Justice Society
www.justicesociety.org

This organization connects people and strategies to advance the cause of justice through social enterprise, advocacy, networking, and consulting.

Love146
www.love146.org

The mission of this US- and UK-based organization is to end child trafficking and exploitation through survivor care, prevention education, and training.

Mission 21
www.mission21mn.org

Mission 21 is an anti-trafficking service provider committed to the complete restoration of child victims of sex trafficking.

National Center for Missing & Exploited Children
www.ncmec.org

For thirty years, NCMEC has been at the forefront of the fight to keep children safe from abduction and sexual exploitation. The organization provides the resources needed to help protect children, bring perpetrators to justice, and prevent these devastating crimes committed against children.

Operation Predator, US Department of Homeland Security
www.ice.gov/predator

Operation Predator is an international initiative to identify, investigate, and arrest child predators who possess, trade, and produce child pornography, travel overseas for sex with minors, and engage in the sex trafficking of children.

Polaris Project
www.polarisproject.org

By successfully pushing for stronger federal and state laws, operating the National Human Trafficking Resource Center hotline (888-373-7888), conducting training, and providing vital services to victims of trafficking, Polaris Project creates long-term solutions that move our society closer to a world without slavery.

PROMISE Model, Salvation Army
www.salarmychicago.org/promise

The Salvation Army developed the PROMISE model (Partnership to Rescue our Minors from Sexual Exploitation) to combat the sexual trafficking of children. This model includes the formation of a task force that engages in initiatives to address the four main provisions of PROMISE: awareness, prevention, intervention, and service delivery.

Refuge City
www.refuge-city.org

Refuge City exists to fund and provide homes of refuge to domestic victims of sexual exploitation and/or sexual human trafficking, serving both children and women.

The SAGE Project
www.sagesf.org

The SAGE Project (Standing Against Global Exploitation) is a primary resource for information about commercial sexual exploitation and human trafficking for sex and labor of both adults and children. SAGE has one of the longest-standing "john school" programs in the country.

Shared Hope International
www.sharedhope.org

Shared Hope International strives to prevent conditions that foster sex trafficking, to restore victims of sex slavery, and bring justice to vulnerable women and children.

Streetlight USA
www.streetlightusa.org

This is a national leader in researching, assessing, and piloting healing methods. The organization's residential program incorporates these healing methods into the girls' care.

Traffick911
www.traffick911.org

This group's mission is to stop the buying and selling of America's children younger than eighteen with a three-pronged, parallel strategy: prevention, rescue, and restoration.

Unlikely Heroes
www.unlikelyheroes.com

This group's mission is to rescue, restore, and rehabilitate child victims of sex slavery through the implementation of restoration homes, rescue, and prevention programs.

World Relief
www.worldrelief.org

World Relief has partnered with local law enforcement to rescue and provide comprehensive services to survivors of human trafficking in the United States. World Relief trains thousands of community members how to identify victims of trafficking every year.

RESOURCES

"And Boys Too," ECPAT-USA, https://static.mopro.
    com/00028B1B-B0DB-4FCD-A991-219527535DAB/1b1293ef-
    1524-4f2c-b148-91db11379d11.pdf.

"Child Sex Trafficking at a Glance," Polaris Project, www.ocwtp.net/
    PDFs/DL/HT/Child_Sex_Trafficking_At_A_Glance.pdf.

"National Report on Domestic Minor Sex Trafficking: America's
    Prostituted Children," Shared Hope International, 2009,
    www.sharedhope.org/wp-content/uploads/2012/09/SHI_National_
    Report_on_DMST_2009.pdf.

"National Strategy for Child Exploitation, Prevention, and Interdiction:
    A Report to Congress," US Department of Justice, 2010, www.
    justice.gov/psc/docs/natstrategyreport.pdf.

"Tools for Service Providers and Law Enforcement," Polaris
    Project, http://www.polarisproject.org/resources/
    tools-for-service-providers-and-law-enforcement.

"Trafficking in Persons Report," US Department of State, www.state.
    gov/j/tip/rls/tiprpt/.

SEX TRAFFICKING DEFINITIONS

Because this book is about the commercial sexual exploitation of children, the terms "victim" and "girl" or "boy" are used in lieu of "prostitute," as the typical definition would state.

I believe that *all* adults and children who have been psychologically and/ or physically lured or forced into prostitution are victims. Although this is a highly debated point of view among trafficking advocates, I also believe that some people who are initially victimized might, at some point, become perpetrators themselves.

Here are some of the most common definitions used in sex trafficking:

Automatic: Refers to a "robotic" state of being induced by severe manipulation, whereby the victim continues to perform sexual favors without being monitored.

Bitch: A term used by pimps, prostitutes/victims, and customers to address or refer to a victim.

Bottom, bottom bitch, or bottom girl: The role of a bottom is considered to be a position of power and status over the other girls under the pimp's control. She may be required to handle finances, train and recruit other girls, work the track in her pimp's stead, run interference for and collect money from the girls under the pimp's control, and look after the pimp's affairs if he is out of town, incarcerated, or otherwise unavailable.

Branding: Pimps often tattoo or brand their names or a symbol ($ or barcode) on the victim's neck, pubic area, chest, or inner thigh to indicate that she is his property. Branding is also commonly done with a shaped, heated coat hanger pressed into the skin to leave a permanent mark.

Breaking: The first time a girl gives all of the money she has earned for the day to a pimp.

Break in or season: When a pimp rapes, beats, manipulates, and intimidates a new recruit or captive to break down.

Bruises: Victims are commonly forced to use makeup to cover bruising on their bodies.

Catcher: Usually a younger "wannabe pimp" paid by a pimp to watch his girls to ensure they are following the pimp's orders.

Caught a case: A term used to indicate that either a pimp or a victim has been arrested and charged with a crime.

Choosing up: When a victim makes direct eye contact with a pimp who does not "own" her, or when another pimp convinces a victim to work for him. The victim has to give her new pimp all of the money she made that evening. Typically, the new pimp will be required to pay the old pimp a negotiated fee for taking his worker.

Commercial sexual exploitation of a child (CSEC): Any situation in which a child is induced to perform sexual acts by a third party who profits. CSEC is the recognized acronym used by law enforcement and governmental agencies.

Couch surfing: Homeless youths' temporary utilization of the home of a friend, family member, or acquaintance for a place to sleep. A common situation for minors who are commercially sexually exploited.

Curb crawling: Driving slowly down the street with the intent to pick up a prostitute.

Daddy: The term victims are often required, or choose, to call their pimp.

Date or trick: A term used to refer to a john or the activity of prostitution—for example, "with a date," "with a trick," "dating," "tricking."

Domestic minor sex trafficking (DMST): A term used when a child younger than eighteen and born in the United States is a victim of trafficking within this country. This term was coined by Shared Hope International.

Exit fee: Money a pimp will demand from a victim who is thinking about trying to leave. It will be an exorbitant sum, to discourage her from leaving. Most pimps never let their victims leave freely.

Family or folk: A group of people under the control of one pimp who plays the role of "father."

Finesse pimp: A pimp who uses psychological manipulation as a primary means of control.

Follow your money: A phrase pimps use to warn victims to take care of the money they are given. Losing money by any means, such as being robbed by a trick, will result in being turned back out to work twenty-four hours a day until the money is replaced and the daily quota also is met.

Fronts or walking-around money: Money a pimp will give his victims to use for cab fare, drinks, and condoms.

Game or The Life: The sex industry in general.

Gorilla pimp: A pimp who uses violence as a primary means of control.

Ho: Short for "whore."

Holine: A loose intercity or interstate network of telephone communication among pimps that is used to trade, buy, and sell women and children. Pimps often use changing slang and code words to confound law enforcement along the "circuit."

Hustler: A male victim, especially for homosexual clients.

In-call: An arrangement to have the john come to a house or apartment for the purpose of purchasing and having sex on-site.

Izz or Izzn: Letters added to words of communication between pimps for the purpose of making law enforcement surveillance difficult and evidence problematic in court cases. When presenting evidence using this slang, prosecutors could be required to provide expert witnesses to translate for the court.

John: One who purchases commercial sex acts, including pornography.

Kiddie stroll or runway: An area of the "track" featuring kids younger than sixteen.

Lay some drag: The words and actions a victim is taught to use when interacting with people not involved in prostitution.

Lick hitter: A severely addicted person who prostitutes just enough to get a dose of drugs or alcohol. When that wears off, the person is back on the "track" until he or she can afford another dose.

Lot lizard: A derogatory term for a prostitute/victim at truck stops. Truck-stop traffickers advertise girls via CB radio or by having girls solicit customers by going truck to truck. Johns signal that they want to purchase sex by using their headlights or a sticker on their windows.

Madam: An older woman who manages a brothel. She may have been a victim in her earlier years but, over time, has become a pimp/career criminal in her own right.

Out of pocket: When a victim speaks, looks at, or makes gestures to another pimp, suggesting she wants to work for him now.

Outcall: An arrangement to have a victim go to or meet a john at a location to provide sexual services.

Outlaw or renegade: Someone who is involved in prostitution without a pimp.

Peel a trick: When a girl or boy steals money, checkbooks, or credit cards from a john. The items may be used by members of a prostitution ring or sold for identity theft.

Pimp: A person who persuades or forces another to engage in prostitution. Typically, a pimp collects all of the money paid by the johns.

Pimp circle: The process of multiple pimps swarming and surrounding one woman or girl and hissing insults at her, for the purpose of humiliation and intimidation.

Pimp hard: A pimp's practice of raising quotas, reducing rest times, and/or requiring a victim to accept dangerous tricks he or she would ordinarily avoid.

Pimp party: When several pimps come together to rape, beat, and drug someone who is resisting being prostituted or who was "out of line" by trying to escape or talking to the police.

Pimp stick: A steel whip made out of coat-hanger wire that may be heated on a stove to brand, burn, or cut the victim.

Player: Another term for "pimp."

Pornography or porn: Sexual activity depicted in words, pictures, or films.

Quota: Most victims are expected to earn a daily quota, generally ranging from $500 to $1,000, that she gives to the pimp. In some cases, pimps demand that a girl service a certain number of men each night as her daily quota.

Rabbit: A victim who goes from one pimp to another too frequently.

Reckless eyeballing: When a girl is engaged in eye contact too long with another pimp or male counterpart and appears interested in his appearance, car, clothes, girls, etc.

Roll a trick: When a victim, pimp, or his associates rob a trick with force. Usually involves weak or intoxicated tricks.

Rufi: A slang term for a powerful sedative drug that is illegal in the United States, commonly known as the "date rape" drug because its ability to cause semiconsciousness and memory blackouts is associated with unwanted sexual encounters.

Senior citizen: A victim older than twenty-four or a pimp in his thirties.

Sex trafficking: The recruitment and/or movement of someone within or across borders, through the abuse of power or position with the intention of sexual exploitation, commercial or otherwise.

Shoes: A victim's shoes are often confiscated to prevent her from running away.

Sister wife, sister-in-law, or wife-in-law: Each individual in a group of women or girls who is with the same pimp.

Sponge: Instead of being allowed to use tampons, victims often are required to cut up pieces of kitchen sponges and insert them in their vaginas to absorb menstrual blood without the johns noticing, as they would with a tampon.

Square: Someone who tries to go straight and get out of the life; law enforcement and others who are not in the lifestyle.

Stable: A group of people under the control of a single pimp.

Staying in pocket: The practice of forbidding a victim from observing street or establishment names or general surroundings during "dates" in an effort to keep them isolated.

Stroll or track: A common area or cross streets where street prostitution is known to occur on a nightly basis.

Tracker: A person who tracks and returns an escaped victim to a pimp for a fee.

Trade up, trade down, buy and sell: These terms refer to a pimp's disposal of victims who are considered difficult or no longer match the profile sought by the clientele the pimp normally serves. The buy/sell price is usually low—$2,500 to $3,500—while the trade value is typically straight across—person for person or one person for two people. The victims are guarded and can be moved long distances rapidly by ground transportation or overnight air.

Trick: A term used to refer to a john or the activity of prostitution.

Turn out: The first sexual act performed by a victim for which money is exchanged.

NOTES

CHAPTER 1—KIDS FOR SALE: A GLOBAL VIEW

1. "Children Out of Sight, Out of Mind, Out of Reach: Abused and Neglected, Millions of Children Have Become Virtually Invisible," UNICEF, December 14, 2005, http://www.unicef.org/media/media_30453.html.

2. "Trafficking in Persons Report 2008," US Department of State, http://www.state.gov/j/tip/rls/tiprpt/2008/; "Child Sex Trafficking," Child Wise, http://childwise.blob.core.windows.net/assets/uploads/files/Fact%20Sheets/About_CSEC.pdf

3. "Child Marriage Facts and Figures," International Center for Research on Women, http://www.icrw.org/child-marriage-facts-and-figures.

4. Charlene Smith, "The Relation between HIV Prevalence and Virgin Rape," The Nordic Africa Institute, http://www.nai.uu.se/publications/news/archives/032smith/.

5. Melissa Hermann (executive director, Courage House), personal interview with the author, November 2013.

CHAPTER 2—IN OUR OWN BACKYARD: CHILD SEX TRAFFICKING IN AMERICA

1. Janet Kornblum, "Child Prostitution Survivor Aims to Change Lives," *USA TODAY*, February 27, 2008, http://usatoday30.usatoday.com/news/nation/2008-02-26-carissa-child-prostitution_N.htm.

2. "FAQs," Shared Hope, May 2009, www.sharedhope.org/learn/faqs/.

3. "Child Exploitation and Obscenity Section," US Department of Justice, http://www.justice.gov/criminal/ceos/.

4. Ian Urbina, "For Runaways, Sex Buys Survival," *The New York Times*, October 26, 2009, http://www.nytimes.com/2009/10/27/us/27runaways.html?pagewanted=all&_r=0.

5. "Victims of Trafficking and Violence Protection Act of 2000: Trafficking in Persons Report," http://www.state.gov/j/tip/rls/tiprpt/2004/.

6. Sara Thomas and Renea Anderson, "Human Trafficking: Modern-Day Slavery," PowerPoint presentation, Georgia Bureau of Investigation, Human Trafficking Unit, http://dfcs.dhs.georgia.gov/sites/dfcs.dhs.georgia.gov/files/related_files/site_page/BST%20Human%20Trafficking%20Workshop.pdf.

7. "Victims of Trafficking and Violence Protection Act of 2000: Trafficking in Persons Report," http://www.state.gov/j/tip/rls/tiprpt/2004/.

8. Linda A. Smith, Samantha Healy Vardaman, and Melissa A. Snow, "The National Report on Domestic Minor Sex Trafficking: America's Prostituted Children," Shared Hope International, May 2009, www.sharedhope.org/wp-content/uploads/2012/09/SHI_National_Report_on_DMST_2009.pdf.

9. "Who Is Involved in Systems of Prostitution?" The Sage Project, http://sagesf.org/who-involved-systems-prostitution; "An Introduction to Human Trafficking: Vulnerability, Impact, and Action," United Nations background paper, Office on Drugs and Crime,2008, http://www.unodc.org/documents/human-trafficking/An_Introduction_to_Human_Trafficking_-_Background_Paper.pdf.

10. Richard J. Estes and Neil Alan Weiner, "The Commercial Sexual Exploitation of Children in the US, Canada, and Mexico." University of Pennsylvania, School of Social Work, February 20, 2002, http://www.sp2.upenn.edu/restes/CSEC_Files/Complete_CSEC_020220.pdf.

11. "Child Exploitation and Obscenity Section," ibid.

12. "South Park Prostitute Song with Lyrics," December 17, 2010, http://www.youtube.com/watch?v=HApbmtryRYk.

13. "Human Trafficking 101 for School Administrators and Staff," US Department of Homeland Security, Blue Campaign, https://www.dhs.gov/sites/default/files/publications/blue-campaign/Blue%20Campaign%20-%20Human%20Trafficking%20101%20for%20School%20Administrators%20and%20Staff.pdf.

14. Estes and Weiner, "ibid; "Pornography Statistics." Family Safe Media, http://familysafemedia.com/pornography_statistics.html.

15. Child Exploitation and Obscenity Section," ibid.

16. Tammy Turon (director of programming, prostitution diversion initiative. Dallas, TX), personal interview with the author, October 16, 2013.

CHAPTER 3—OVERVIEW: LOVER BOY SYNDROME

1. Jody Raphael and Brenda Meyers–Powell, "From Victims to Victimizers: Interviews with Twenty-Five Ex-Pimps in Chicago," DePaul College of Law, a report from the Schiller DuCanto & Fleck Family Law Center of DePaul University College of Law, September 2010, http://newsroom.depaul.edu/pdf/family_law_center_report-final.pdf.

2. Ibid.

3. "Child Trafficking Survivor Shares Her Story," HuffPost Live, article and video, July30, 2013, http://www.huffingtonpost.com/2013/07/30/child-trafficking_n_3678465.html.

4. "Domestic Sex Trafficking: The Criminal Operations of the American Pimp," Polaris Project, print. n.d.

5. "Sarah: Domestic Minor Sex Trafficking," Polaris Project, http://www.polarisproject.org/what-we-do/client-services/survivor-stories/465-sarah-domestic-minor-sex-trafficking.

6. D. G. Dutton and S. L. Painter, "Traumatic Bonding: The Development of Emotional Bonds in Relationships of Intermittent Abuse," *Victimology: An International Journal* 6, 1–4 (1981): 139–55.

7. Pimpin' Ken and Hunter, *Pimpology 101: The Forty-Eight Laws of the Game* (New York: Simon Spotlight Entertainment, 2007).

8. Donna M. Hughes, "Tattoos of Girls under Pimp Control and Pimp Rules for the Control of Victims," August 10, 2009, Citizens Against Trafficking, http://www.citizensagainsttrafficking.com/uploads/Tattoos_and_Control_of_Victims.pdf.

9. Raphael and Meyers–Powell, ibid.

10. Pimpin' Ken and Hunter, ibid.

11. "Child Exploitation and Obscenity Section," ibid; Thomas and Anderson, ibid; Smith, Vardaman, and Snow, ibid.

12. Jacqueline Rabe Thomas, "Recruiting a Child Prostitute in Connecticut," *The CT Mirror*, August 6, 2012, http://www.ctmirror.org/story/2012/08/03/recruiting-child-prostitute-connecticut.

13. "Child Exploitation and Obscenity Section," ibid; Thomas and Anderson, ibid.

14. "FY 2011 Budget Request at a Glance," Federal Bureau of Investigation, http://www.justice.gov/jmd/2011summary/pdf/fy11-fbi-bud-summary.pdf.

15. Mia Spangenberg, "Prostituted Youth in New York City: An Overview," ECPAT-USA, 2001, http://ecpatusa.org/wp/wp-content/uploads/2013/08/Prostituted-Youth-in-NYC.pdf.

16. United States v. Pipkins. No. 02-14306, US Court of Appeals for the Eleventh Circuit, August 2, 2004, http://www.ca11.uscourts.gov/opinions/ops/200214306.pdf.

17. Raphael and Meyers–Powell, ibid.

CHAPTER 4—OVERVIEW: FAMILIAL TRAFFICKING

1. Ibid.

2. Brandon Herring, "Antoinette Davis reaches plea deal," *WNCN*, November 1, 2013, http://www.wncn.com/story/23728590/judge-rules-antoinette-davis-statements-can-be-used.

3. Brian Rogers, "Houston Girl Says Family Forced Her into Prostitution," *Houston Chronicle*, August 12, 2010, http://www.chron.com/news/houston-texas/article/Houston-girl-says-family-forced-her-into-1699524.php.

4. Raphael and Meyers–Powell, ibid.

5. "Child Sex Trafficking at a Glance," Polaris Project, http:// http://www.polarisproject.org/resources/resources-by-topic/sex-trafficking.

6. Kimberly Tyler and Ana Mari Cauce, "Perpetrators of Early Physical and Sexual Abuse among Homeless and Runaway Adolescents," University of Nebraska–Lincoln Sociology Department, Faculty Publications, December 1, 2002, http://digitalcommons.unl.edu/cgi/viewcontent.cgi?article=1054&context=sociologyfacpub.

7. Kristin M. Finklea, Adrienne L. Fernandes–Alcantara, and Alison Siskin, "Sex Trafficking of Children in the United States: Overview and Issues for Congress," Federation of American Scientists website, Congressional Search Service, CRS Report for Congress, June 21, 2011, http://www.fas.org/sgp/crs/misc/R41878.pdf.

8. Nicki Rossoll, "Foster Care and Sex Trafficking Survivor Testifies on Hill," ABC News, October 23, 2013, http://abcnews.go.com/blogs/politics/2013/10/foster-care-and-sex-trafficking-survivor-testifies-on-hill/.

9. Smith, Vardaman, and Snow, ibid.

10. Senate Bill S.1118, Child Sex Trafficking Data and Response Act of 2013, 113th Congress, June 7, 2013, http://beta.congress.gov/bill/113th/senate-bill/1118.

CHAPTER 5—OVERVIEW: SURVIVAL SEX AND MALE EXPLOITATION

1. Brahami Houston, "Survival Sex: Why Many Homeless Youth Barter Sex for Necessities," *The Portland Mercury*, December 7, 2000, http://www.portlandmercury.com/portland/survival-sex/Content?oid=23504.

2. Estes and Weiner, ibid.; "Bought and Sold: Helping Young People Escape from Commercial Sexual Exploitation," National Clearinghouse on Families and Youth, US Department of Health and Human Services, http://ncfy.acf.hhs.gov/sites/default/files/bought_and_sold.pdf.

3. "Runaway and Homeless Youth and Relationship Violence Toolkit," National Resource Center on Domestic Violence, http://www.nrcdv.org/rhydvtoolkit/.

4. Estes and Weiner, ibid.

5. R. B. Flowers, *Runaway Kids and Teenage Prostitution*, (Westport, CT: Praeger Publishers, 2001).

6. K. Kaye, "Sex and the Unspoken in Male Street Prostitution," *Journal of Homosexuality*, 53, 1–2 (2007).

7. "Homelessness, Survival Sex, and Human Trafficking: As Experienced by Youth at Covenant House New York," Covenant House, May 2013, http://www.covenanthouse.org/sites/default/files/attachments/Covenant-House-trafficking-study.pdf.

8. R. Curtis, K. Terry, M. Dank, K. Dombrowski, and B. Khan, "The Commercial Sexual Exploitation of Children in New York City, Volume One, The CSEC Population in New York City: Size, Characteristics, and Needs," Center for Court Innovation and John Jay College of Criminal Justice. (2008):115; Sgt. Chris Bray (City of Phoenix Police Department, Drug Enforcement Bureau Vice Enforcement Unit), personal interview with the author, June 2010.

9. Curtis, Terry, Dank, Dombrowski, and Khan, ibid.

10. Estes and Weiner, ibid.

11. J. M. Edwards, B. J. Iritani, and D. D. Hallfors, Prevalence and Correlates of Exchanging Sex for Drugs or Money among Adolescents in the United States: Sexually Transmitted Infections. 82, no. 5 (2005): 354-8.

12. Brian Willis, Norene Robert, and Sara Ann Friedman, "And Boys Too: An ECPAT-USA Discussion Paper about the Lack of Recognition of the Commercial Sexual Exploitation of Boys in the United States," ECPAT-USA, 2013, http://ecpatusa.org/wp/wp-content/uploads/2013/08/AndBoysToo_FINAL_single-pages.pdf.

13. "Ventnor Man Arrested on Charges He Ran Human Trafficking and Male Prostitution Ring out of His Apartment," press release, The State of New Jersey, Department of Law and Public Safety, Office of the Attorney General. October 22, 2012, http://www.nj.gov/oag/newsreleases12/pr20121022a.html.

14. Willis, Robert, and Friedman, ibid.

15. K. Kaye, ibid.

16. Sgt. Chris Bray interview, ibid.

17. "Male Victims of Sex Trafficking," Toy Soldiers blog, May 17, 2011, http://toysoldier.wordpress.com/2012/10/25/male-victims-of-sex-trafficking/.

18. Willis, Robert, and Friedman, ibid.

CHAPTER 6—OVERVIEW: RECRUITMENT TACTICS

1. Estes and Weiner, ibid.

2. Colin Smith, "FBI Ranks Minnesota 13th in US for Sex Trafficking," CBS Minnesota, June 12, 2013, http://minnesota.cbslocal.com/2013/06/12/fbi-ranks-minnesota-13th-in-u-s-for-sex-trafficking/.

3. Attiyya Anthony, "Innocence Lost," *The Crime Report*, July 24, 2012, http://www.thecrimereport.org/news/inside-criminal-justice/2012-07-innocence-lost.

4. Raphael and Meyers–Powell, ibid.

5. Mia Spangenberg, "Prostituted Youth in New York City: An Overview," ECPAT-USA, 2001, http://ecpatusa.org/wp/wp-content/uploads/2013/08/Prostituted-Youth-in-NYC.pdf.

6. "Child Sex Trafficking at a Glance," ibid.

7. "Domestic Sex Trafficking: The Criminal Operations of the American Pimp," ibid.

8. Abby Simons, "Hopkins Woman Who Prostituted Fellow Cheerleader Sentenced," *Star Tribune*, October 11, 2013, http://www.startribune.com/local/west/227398191.html.

9. "Internet Based," Polaris Project, http://www.polarisproject.org/human-trafficking/sex-trafficking-in-the-us/internet-based.

10. "Online Prostitution-Ad Revenue Crosses Craigslist Benchmark," Aim Group, July 10, 2013, http://aimgroup.com/2013/07/10/online-prostitution-ad-revenue-crosses-craigslist-benchmark/.

11. "Child Exploitation and Obscenity Section," ibid.

12. "Internet Based," Polaris Project, http://www.polarisproject.org/human-trafficking/sex-trafficking-in-the-us/internet-based.

13. The Rebecca Project for Human Rights, July 2010, http://www.rebeccaproject.org/dearcraig/Dear_Craig.pdf.

14. Doe v. MySpace, 528 F.3d 413, US Court of Appeals, Fifth Circuit, filed May 16, 2008, http://www.ca5.uscourts.gov/opinions/pub/07/07-50345-CV0.wpd.pdf.

15. Anthony, ibid.

16. "Gang Criminal Activity Expanding into Juvenile Prostitution Intelligence Report," National Gang Intelligence Center & FBI's Crimes against Children Unit, January 31, 2012, http://www.goccp.maryland.gov/victim/documents/human-trafficking/research-policy/Gang-Criminal-Activity-Expanding-Into-Juvenile-Prostitution.pdf.

17. George D. Knox, "Females and Gangs: Sexual Violence, Prostitution, and Exploitation," abstract, National Criminal Justice Reference Service, 2008, https://www.ncjrs.gov/App/publications/abstract.aspx?ID=206498.

18. US v. Michael Tavon Jefferies, Case No. 1:12-cr-143,US District Court, Eastern District of Virginia, July 6, 2012, http://s3.amazonaws.com/content.washingtonexaminer.biz/documents/MichaelJefferies-sentencingmemo.pdf.

19. *The Shawshank Redemption*, movie quote, 1994, http://www.imdb.com/title/tt0111161/quotes.

20. Smith, Vardaman, and Snow, ibid; "Domestic Sex Trafficking: The Criminal Operations of the American Pimp," ibid.

21. Cathy Brock (director, Dallas Community High Risk Victims Task Force, retired; residential supervisor, Letot Girls' Center), telephone interview with the author, November 14, 2013.

22. "Operation Cross Country: Recovering Victims of Child Sex Trafficking," Federal Bureau of Investigation. July 29, 2013, http://www.fbi.gov/news/stories/2013/july/operation-cross-country-recovering-victims-of-child-sex-trafficking.

23. "The National Strategy for Child Exploitation Prevention and Interdiction: A Report to Congress," US Department of Justice, August 2010, http://www.justice.gov/psc/docs/natstrategyreport.pdf.

24. Smith, Vardaman, and Snow, ibid; "Domestic Sex Trafficking: The Criminal Operations of the American Pimp," ibid.

25. Nicholas D. Kristof, "She Has a Pimp's Name Etched on Her," *The New York Times*, "The Opinion Pages," May 23, 2012, http://www.nytimes.com/2012/05/24/opinion/kristof-she-has-a-pimps-name-etched-on-her.html?_r=0.

26. Jessica Lustig, "The Thirteen-Year-Old Prostitute: Working Girl or Sex Slave?" *New York* magazine website, "News & Politics" section, October 24, 2007, http://nymag.com/news/features/30018/.

27. Estes and Weiner, ibid; "2012 Domestic Sex Trafficking in Ohio," Ohio Attorney General, August 8, 2012, https://www.ohioattorneygeneral.gov/OhioAttorneyGeneral/files/2f/2ff15706-77ad-4567-b1aa-d8330b5c4005.pdf.

28. "*American Pimp* Movie Quotes," Humble Genius, http://www.humblegeni.us/1471-American-Pimp-Quotes.qt.

29. "Oakland Prostitutes Being Forced to Rob Clients, Police Sting Reveals," CBS, May 23, 2013, http://sanfrancisco.cbslocal.com/2013/05/23/oakland-prostitutes-being-forced-to-rob-clients-police-sting-reveals/.

30. "Domestic Sex Trafficking: The Criminal Operations of the American Pimp," ibid; "Glossary of Trafficking Terms," Shared Hope International, http://sharedhope.org/learn/traffickingterms/.

CHAPTER 6—STORY: THE SETUP

1. "Sex Trafficking at Truck Stops." Polaris Project, http://www.polarisproject.org/human-trafficking/sex-trafficking-in-the-us/truck-stops.

CHAPTER 7—OVERVIEW: KIDNAPPING

1. "Human Trafficking Trends in the United States: National Human Trafficking Resource Center 2007–2012," Polaris Project. November 21, 2013, http://www.polarisproject.org/resources/hotline-statistics/human-trafficking-trends-in-the-united-states.

2. "Teen Girls' Stories of Sex Trafficking in US," ABC News. February 9, 2006, http://abcnews.go.com/Primetime/story?id=1596778.

3. David Finkelhor and Richard Ormrod, "Characteristics of Crimes against Juveniles." *Juvenile Justice Bulletin.* December 3, 2013.

4. Sun Tzu, *The Art of War* (Boston: Shambhala Publications, 1988).

CHAPTER 8—YOU DON'T HAVE TO BE A ROCK STAR: EVERYDAY PEOPLE MAKING A DIFFERENCE

1. Joshua McAfee (founder, McAfee Institute), e-mail interview with the author, November 10, 2013.

2. Alexia La Benz and Gina La Benz (GS GEMS), e-mail and telephone interview with the author, November 10, 2013.

3. Dr. Dina Hijazi (licensed specialist in school psychology, Dallas Independent School District, Dallas, TX), e-mail interview with the author, November 10, 2013.

4. "A Mother's Day Gift to Stop Child Trafficking," Sprittibee blog, April 27, 2010, http://sprittibee.com/2010/04.

5. Kelly Master, "Call 2 Action: Removal of Child Sex Dolls," Dining for Dignity, November 22, 2013, http://diningfordignity.org/call-2-action-removal-of-child-sex-dolls/.

6. Dr. Sophia Grant (child abuse pediatrician, Cooks Children's Hospital), telephone interview, November 2013.

INDEX

A

abduction   173, 231

age   9-10, 15-16, 26, 63, 68-71, 76, 83, 85, 97, 103, 105, 107, 137, 139-140, 173

ages   9, 15-16, 64, 106, 137, 139, 167

automatic   24-25, 235

B

bisexual   106

bonding   22-23, 25, 142, 245

bottom   28, 42, 49, 78, 162, 188, 211, 235

Branch, Marc   106

branding   141-142, 224, 235

brother   31, 89, 105, 146, 160, 176

brothers   105, 146-147, 158-159, 171

C

child sex trafficking   ix, xi, 1-3, 9-10, 13-18, 63, 66, 139-140, 173, 209, 211, 215, 217-220, 227, 234, 243, 246-247, 249-250

commercial sexual exploitation of a child (CSEC)   236

Craigslist   139, 184, 195, 203, 249

D

Daddy   77, 94, 105, 111-112, 128, 139, 161-162, 188, 236

Domestic Minor Sex Trafficking (DMST)   14, 217, 236

F

family   ii, 7-9, 15, 18, 25, 32, 59, 62-68, 76, 81, 84-85, 91, 97, 105, 113, 134, 139, 141, 146, 155, 163, 166-169, 172, 174, 176, 183, 185, 197, 202, 205, 208-209, 236-237, 245-246

T

V

JUSTICE CAN BE CONTAGIOUS

Help us spread Justice Society's message of "Hate evil. Love good. Do justice."

Here are some practical and helpful things you can do to end the injustice of child sex trafficking in America:

✓ Purchase a 10-pack of *Made in the USA* to give away to your friends. Go to our website, click "Buy the Book" for special pricing. Or, just order copies on line through Amazon.com or visit your local bookstore to order copies.

✓ Visit the Justice Society's website, www.JusticeSociety.org, and donate your time, talent or treasure to help end injustice worldwide.

✓ Write a positive review or comment about *Made in the USA* on your blog, Twitter, and Facebook page.

✓ Suggest *Made in the USA* to friends and colleagues.

✓ When you're in a bookstore, ask if they carry the book. The book is available through all major distributors, so any bookstore that does not have it in stock can easily order it.

✓ Write a positive review of the book on www.amazon.com.

VOLUNTEER TO END INJUSTICE

THERE ARE 27 MILLION people in the world with no voice, no hope, and no one to turn to. Are you part of a group, church, club or network of justice minded individuals committed to responsibly addressing an issue of social injustice? Justice Society welcomes impassioned people to help make a difference through numerous volunteer opportunities. To find out how you can make a difference, just log on to www.**JusticeSociety.org** and connect with one of the committed organizations in need of your help.

MORE WAYS TO SPREAD JUSTICE

Yorlene, Elena & Gisele are three courageous woman with a plan to start a small baking business. When asked their motivation for starting the business, they replied "to feed our children." These women come from a dangerous, impoverished community where a vision for the future is seldom discussed. These women saw a vision for a hopeful future. Tirrases, Costa Rica Feb 2013.

MICRO–BUSINESS OPPORTUNITIES

JUSTICE SOCIETY WORKS HAND in hand with families and communities to create and grow small businesses through business development, education and micro-loans.

Around the world, many women and young girls work in the red light districts because they do not see any other way to provide income for their families. We know there is a better way—and we are committed to providing opportunities and solutions so they can be FREE.

Join Justice Society in providing micro-business opportunities for those living in high-risk and red light districts around the world.

When you give to the Justice Society Micro-business Fund on **www.JusticeSociety.org**, your donations will be used for micro-loans, business development, education and training for those desiring and committed to start a better life.

SOCIAL ENTERPRISE

JUSTICE SOCIETY WORKS WITH international communities to provide social enterprise such as medical services, educational programs and community projects. Our commitment is to provide services through local agencies that benefit and meet the needs of a community.

In 2013, Justice Society partnered to support a medical camp in Bihar India providing free medicine for colds and infections, general check-ups, screenings and tests by certified physicians. Aids screening and awareness was particularly important, as this community was located in the red light district.

LEARN MORE ABOUT SPREADING JUSTICE

Have Alisa Jordheim, Founder and Executive Director of Justice Society, speak at your college, church or event. Alisa's work spans multiple nations and social issues, but her focus is clear: She stands against injustice and empowers others to do the same. Keynote topics can include:

- International sex trafficking
- Sex trafficking within the US
- At-risk communities
- Micro-loan programs

To book Alisa for your next event, email **info@justicesociety.org**.